Woven Bliss

By

Yvonne Bloor

Copyright © 2025 Yvonne Bloor

ISBN: 978-1-918264-88-3

All rights reserved, including the right to reproduce this book, or portions thereof in any form. No part of this text may be reproduced, transmitted, downloaded, decompiled, reverse engineered, or stored, in any form or introduced into any information storage and retrieval system, in any form or by any means, whether electronic or mechanical without the express written permission of the author.

This is a work of fiction. Names and characters are the product of the author's imagination and any resemblance to actual persons, living or dead, is entirely coincidental.

Acknowledgements

I am grateful as always to my best bud June Shaw for assisting me in the reading out loud of the final novel of the Gibson Family. It brought so much joy to see how the Novel developed.

In addition, I would like to give a Big Thank you to my best bud June Shaw for recreating the front cover of the book, with its illuminating effect that emulates part of the storyline.

To my dearest friend Leonora, I thank you for your huge support and encouragement.

I would like to thank my beautiful Daughter Sarah, and my lovely son-in-law Keith, as always, who have always been encouraging and supportive of my novel writing.

A big thank you to my Tutors, Norma Shaw, Sociology, and Francine Price, Psychology at Cauldon College in Stoke back in 2002, of whom I wouldn't have been able to create a character like Hazel in my Novel.

Yvonne Bloor

Chapter 1

As Jacqueline sat in the window box in Jason's library at the rear of his lovely country home. She nestled herself on the window box with a large cushion underneath her legs and watched the season of spring come alive with its wealth of growth, as the plants and flower beds came out of their hibernation.

The freshness of the air and the wispy breeze how it swaggered along the leafy stems of the daisies. They were assembled neatly as a centrepiece near the oak tree which was embedded in the middle of the garden.

She couldn't help but wonder where the yuletide festivities had gone, it seemed like yesterday to her when all the family were gathered here to celebrate Christmas. She gave out a little yawn of appreciation through the window and lifted her arms above her shoulders as she felt Jason's arms around her.

'You look a picture my love, I couldn't help but admire you from the other side of the room' as he gave her a sly wink.

Jacqueline was bemused as she coyly turned to him with a curious look on her face. 'So, you were admiring me from afar were you, and how long was that for I wonder?'

Jason squeezed her waist and smiled,

'It was long enough to know that I cannot wait for you to be my bride' Jacqueline leaped off the window box and said,

'What are you saying, are you proposing to me?'

Jason got down on one knee and asked the important question she was waiting with anticipation....,

'Jacqueline, would you make me the happiest man alive and become my wife' She waivered a moment and walked across the room and replied rather calmly,

'I am not saying no Jason, but can we wait awhile, I need to get my head around this, please don't be upset, it's just I need more time, this is such a big step'

Jason stood in disappointment, as he walked past her and said rather quietly in her ear,

'You take all the time you need; I am off to give Jasper his morning walk, see you later'

He slumped out of the room and shouted! 'Jasper', rather abruptly, as he grabbed his harness. Jasper jumped towards his master, and they walked towards the hilltops. He kept on walking for hours and Jasper was barking loudly as he was getting rather hungry.

'Oh Jasper, I am so sorry lad, I am not myself', as he bent down to stroke his head softly, let's get you home'

Jacqueline at this time had made lunch and was packed to go back to her cottage, she was getting worried but wanted to stay on to explain to Jason that she needed to go home and have a good think.

Jason entered the kitchen and grabbed Jasper's food and drink and took it into the garden as it was a beautiful day. Jacqueline gathered her thoughts and made her way into the garden and shouted to Jason,

'I have made us some lunch dear; in the hope he would join her.

As they sat at the kitchen table Jason gathered his thoughts and looked up at Jacqueline before saying,

'Would you like me to leave you be for a few days or more to think over of my proposal'

She said yes and smiled back at him with a rather grateful look in her eyes. The journey home was quiet somewhat as they listened to some classical music on the radio which was rather relaxing.

As they got out of the car, he took her overnight case to the door and kissed her gently on the cheek and left.

Jacqueline was taken back for a moment but realised that it was probably the best thing.

She slipped her key into the front door and waved Jason off; he didn't look back.... as his was eyes were firmly fixed on the car door. He quickly drove off. As she stood in the doorway she felt a shudder, the presence of her late husband Declan seemed to resonate in the hallway.

Jacqueline dropped her bag and case in the hallway and made her way to the kitchen and as she was putting the kettle on, she began to cry out loud.

'Oh Declan, what is it, what is it with me and you, I cannot seem to let you go completely, it's been so long'

She sat herself down and wiped her tears. Niamh entered the kitchen and walked towards her mam with a concerned look on her face.

'I heard a cry mam, was that you, what is going on mam?'

Jacqueline began telling Niamh what had occurred that morning. Niamh couldn't believe what she was hearing; she couldn't help but feel a little dismayed. She always knew that this would come one day, but she didn't expect Jason to propose so soon, it was a little too soon perhaps...

'Do you know what I think mam, I think you should take time out and have a good think about everything as you are not ready to take such a big step.... I can see it in your face'

Jacqueline hugged her daughter and began slowly saying,

'I am so happy in the moment, but I know in my heart I am not ready for this. I cannot get your father out of my mind, I don't feel comfortable enough to let him go, I just cannot explain it'

Niamh made her mam a cup of tea and they both decided to change the subject. Jacqueline would concentrate on her job teaching the adults down at the Adult Centre, it was however going to be a big week before spring break.

They sat talking for some time and the conversation had sped away from the emotional topic of marriage as Niamh animated her mam through the art of literature and learning because she knew she loved it as much as herself.

Jacqueline at this point became jovial and was looking forward to a week of poetry and short stories with her mature students.

Niamh too, was looking forward to her teaching career, she was elevated with the prospect of becoming Lead in the English Department, it was demanding but she was up for the task. Although Jack, her loving boyfriend, was not, he was hoping for quality time with her.

His plans were also signalling towards a hopeful engagement, but he hadn't plucked the courage up to ask her, nor was he when she announced her good news about her promotion the night before...

It was trying time for the Jason and Jack, but more so for Jason, as he had inadvertently made plans... A honeymoon destination to Italy... He felt so sure Jacqueline would have said yes!

He directly cancelled such a booking and made his way to the hospital although he wasn't on shift but needed to be there to keep himself busy. There was admin to catch up on, and he was happy to be distracted.

His Theatre assistant Hazel was on duty and was so surprised to see him in the hospital. She was very happy to have his presence before her, as she was secretly in love with him but kept her emotions to herself. She quickly moved towards him along the corridor to ask if he needed assistance. Jason was rather curt towards her and brushed quickly past her towards his office.

He slammed his door and savagely brushed his dark hair back from his forehead and grunted

'I won't allow this to interfere with my work, I will put Jacqueline out of my mind as if I hadn't set eyes on her', he grunted a little more and pulled some files open to continue writing his notes on some of his forthcoming patients who were scheduled for surgery the day after.

Hazel made her with to the theatre with a distraught look on her face, and her colleague Alex asked if she was alright, she answered in a rather quiet manner,

'I am alright, it was just something in my eye, nothing to worry about'.

Meanwhile Jacqueline was back in her old routine, she was expecting Colm home for tea, and Bernadette, his fiancé, was accompanying him.

A steak dinner will be had for all, as Jacqueline quickly made her way to the local butchers, it was spritely walk, and she was back to feeling herself once again.

As she walked into the shop, she was met by Simon, one of Declan's old pit colleagues, she was taken back somewhat with his presence as she hadn't seen him since the pit explosion, it seemed an age ago.

They made friendly conversation, the usual how is everyone. Eventually they said their goodbyes, and Jacqueline's mind was set right back to the past as her thoughts and feelings were once again consumed by her late husband. She ached for him at that moment… as she slowly walked home along the coast road.

The sea air was getting chilly now as it was almost 5pm. As she began to hurry along, she realized she couldn't marry again, she couldn't, she wouldn't, it was a lovely episode in her life, but she wasn't prepared to carry on seeing Jason, she had made her mind up, but had she, as she felt so confused a lot of the time.

'I will give myself lots of time and space, that's what I will do', as she talked to herself along the road towards the cottage gate…

Niamh had already set the table ready for her mam returning and it wasn't long after that Colm and Bernadette had made an entrance.

As they all sat around the dining table, Colm asked about Jason and Jacqueline stammered a little and Colm was quick to pick up on this and asked the question,

'What is going on mam, you are acting rather oddly, has something happened'

Jacqueline spurted it out and Colm was surprised, but he wasn't too sure why his mam hadn't accepted. He felt Jason was a lovely man and wanted his mam to be happy.

Niamh on the other hand was only too happy that her mam was giving it a lot of thought before committing to such a big step.

The conversation got rather heated at some point, as Colm began questioning his mam's motives. Jacqueline shouted back and put a stop to it as she changed the subject completely as she wasn't having any of it...

The evening ended abruptly, and Colm took Bernadette out of the house as they ventured to the local pub. Jacqueline was saddened by such an unhappy evening as she wanted it to be a good family gathering, joyful and full of happy conversation...

Niamh sat with her mam and quickly responded by saying,

'Colm's mouth speaks before his brain in his gear mam, he didn't mean to sound so rude, he will think on it and say sorry, he always does when he speaks out of turn, you know that'.

Jacqueline sighed,

'Yes, I know, my son, he is like is dad, a bull in a China shop'

It became a sombre night, and Jacqueline took to her room and read some Emily Dickinson poetry to soothe her aching heart. She quietly drifted off to sleep with the book resting under her arm…

Chapter 2

A wistful longing came upon Jason on this Monday morning at the beginning of April in 1970. He was struggling to get his day going as he bathed and prepared for his big day at the hospital. As he stared at his unshaven face through the bathroom cabinet window, he began giving himself a strong pep talk.

'I will leave her to her own devices, she can come to me, yes', as he tried to convince himself that he was doing ok. He quickly shaved and got dressed and confidently strolled to his car. He was in his doctor's mode, and no one would disturb his excellence, at least not until the evening hours.

Niamh and Jacqueline were all set for their day teaching. They gathered their school bags full of papers and as they did so, Colm brushed passed them in a hurry to his place of work at the shipyard in the Draughtsman office. He gently put his arm on his mam's shoulder and gave her gentle kiss on cheek as he whispered,

'See you tonight mam, love you'

Jacqueline gave him a loving squeeze and waved him off. Niamh smiled back at her brother with a cheeky wink. She escorted her mam to her car and as she drove off Jacqueline began the conversation by saying that she was going to concentrate on the family, as she poured out her feelings and emotions which were contrasting to say the least.

Niamh was silent for a moment as she was concerned about her mother's state of mind, it was as if she had gone backwards. Not to mention the ordeal with the horrible Professor only a year ago… Perhaps it's best that she takes a break from any romantic attachments, as Niamh silently thought this through in her own mind.

'I think that is a good idea mam, you need a break from such delicate situations, family is the best medicine. Afterall, we are the best family aren't we...' as she gives her mam a coy look.

Jacqueline reciprocated, as she curved her mouth sideways and laughed sarcastically as she spoke.

'The best family are we now, such expectations to live up to'

Niamh made sure the banter continued all the way to school; by the time they had arrived they were both in a jovial mood, which continued through the day. Even the students were upbeat all day. It turned out to be a delightful day all round.

Jason, however, was not having the best day; his first operation was cancelled, and it put him in a bad mood. The staff hadn't seen such behaviour from him as he was so composed most of the time…

His day ended on a sour note as he had upset his assistant Hazel, and he was not pleased with himself at all. He gave himself a talking to as he drove home and vowed to put things right the next day.

As he entered his farmhouse totally ashamed of himself. Jasper greeted him with his loving eyes. It seemed to calm him somewhat as he grabbed his harness and took him for his usual long walk.

They went over the brow of the hill and onto the cliff tops that overlooked the local lake. The shimmering light glowed over the surface of the water as it drizzled lightly in the quiet breeze. He sat on the bench nearby and stroked Jasper.

Jason began dwelling on his awful day and he decided he would not let Jacqueline take over his life. She would have to do the running from now on. He was determined to put his work first from now on.

Jacqueline on the other hand, was feeling excited about the prospect of the last semester of which all her mature students will be contemplating a new direction in their life as they get their overall results in July.

She was so proud of them all for doing so well, even those who had not achieved as much as they wanted to, but Jacqueline encouraged them to believe that they had learned so much and gained so much knowledge which they hadn't known before. It was an achievement. She brought the best out of them as she was so passionate about teaching.

The doorbell rang and in walked Emily and Frankie, they had news, such marvellous news! Frankie couldn't contain himself and just spurted it out.

'We're pregnant, can you believe that'

Emily shoved him in the back as she replied with a big smile on her face.

'We are having a baby, yes, and it is I that is pregnant', as she hugged her mam so tightly.

Jacqueline sat down and asked all the usual questions,

'How far along are you'

Emily smiled back at her mam,

'I just got confirmation this morning and I am eight weeks'

Jacqueline put the kettle on and couldn't believe it; she was going to be a grandmother. Oh, how she longed for Declan at that moment as she recalled a conversation long ago when they were lying in bed talking about their children's future and what it would be like to be grandparents.

She let out a small cry at that moment as she watched the boiling kettle. She quickly dried the tears off her cheek and began setting the tray with tea and cake. The Dundee cake was quickly taken out of its wrapper.

'Oh, Dundee cake!' as Frankie said out loud, it was his favourite.

Niamh came down the stairs,

'What is going on in here?', as she brushed past Frankie.

Emily got up to walk towards her sister as she grabbed her hand, 'I am going to have a baby our Niamh'

Niamh's eyes welled up as she kissed her dear sister, 'Oh, our Emily, I am so happy for you and Frankie'

There was not a dry eye in the house, as they watched Colm enter the room, he too, was taken back with such joy.

Niamh asked about the haberdashery and wool shop, and who was going to take over?

'Belinda, of course, she has been a loyal assistant and has learned so much this past year. I am going to get her an assistant; it's all sorted out. Auntie Aileen will oversee everything and keep me informed. As Emily spoke in confident manner.

Niamh gasped out loud,

'You have certainly thought this through our Emily, get you girl. You will be a wonderful mother'

Emily looked tearful once again,

'Oh, sis, you always know how to make me cry'
Enough of all this crying, let's have some music on as Colm strolled over to the radiophone and selected his choice, 'It's a wonderful world'. He was feeling rather chuffed with himself to have selected a fitting song for the occasion.

Colm made his way to the telephone to give his Uncle Dylan a call, and while he was sitting at the telephone table, he decided to call his Aunties Aileen and Sara as it was a big family occasion now. They all arrived simultaneously. Dylan and Serena had brought the twins along, Ethan and Amy.

Frankie looked at the twins, as they were both trying to crawl across the room, they were almost five months now.

He felt a sense of overwhelming joy as he squeezed Emily's hand.

Emily went to sit by Serena to gain some healthy tips her. She wanted everything just right for when the time comes… for the baby to be born….

They talked incessantly for an hour as the others made their way into the kitchen. Colm, Dylan, and Frankie grabbed a beer out of the fridge and made their way into the garden. Frankie too was anxious to get some healthy tips from Dylan. Dylan's response was,

'There is no real guidebook, it's just your pure instinct and you learn as you go along. You have the professionals coming to see you when you leave hospital for the first few months, and you take on board their suggestions. You find your own way to bond with your baby and sleep when you can mate; you will get used to the night- time feeds, take them in turn'.

Frankie looked a little dazed, but Dylan assured him you will know when the time comes mate, call on me anytime as they sipped their beer. They both teased Colm about his future with Bernadette and his response was,

'Give me a chance mate, we are getting married in the summer in August actually. We haven't organized it yet, that's why I haven't said anything, just waiting on Bernadette to say where. She doesn't fancy a church wedding, that's why I haven't said anything because of mam, you what I mean'

Dylan looked straight at him and spoke,

'It's yours and Bernadette's day mate. I am sure Jacqueline will be alright about it, you know, she is not that cruel. She loves her Catholic Church, but she has always been kind and supportive to others who are not religious'

Colm murmured a little,

'Yea, you probably right, let's just get it sorted before anyone says anything'.

It was agreed that it was their secret for now. Dylan jumped up,

'I think this calls from another beer'

Niamh curiously looked out of the window suspecting something was going on, she was so astute. As Colm knew that already, he gazed at her.

'So, boys, what's going on out here then' Frankie butted in,

'We are getting in some practice of wetting the baby's head' as he candidly gave Niamh a sly wink.

'Oh, you are, are you', as Niamh smirked at them from the back door of the cottage.

She wasn't convinced; there was something about Colm's stance and his eyes avoiding her that gave it away. She knew her brother inside out, but she will leave it for now... for today anyway... She loved to probe, nothing got passed Niamh and Colm knew that already....

The night was upon them, and the twins were getting grumpy now, as they were tired. It was time to call it a night. Hugs and kisses all around....

Colm ran up the stairs quickly before Niamh could spot him, he wasn't prepared to get into that conversation, as he knew she would prise it out of him. He quickly got undressed and jumped into the bed.

He could hear footsteps on the landing and a pause, but they seemingly disappeared, he sighed with a relieved look on his face...

Chapter 3

Emily lay in her bed, it was an unusual cool night for May, as the temperatures dipped down to single figures 9c. Frankie lay beside her, he was fast asleep snoring away, as his day had been very busy in the garage.

She sat up in bed contemplating how she was to give up work completely, after all she was the owner.

'Maybe I can go back part time after the first year. I need to speak to mam to ask her thoughts on the subject', she said to herself.

The next day Emily was up and out early. She had decided to leave Belinda in charge. The Adult Centre was a ten-minute walk. She would leave the car behind, as there were no parking spaces. Half of the mature students had cars, and it was always packed. She knew her mam had a break at 10.45am.

As she went through the double doors the receptionist directed her to the teacher's break room. She opened the door, and her mam swung around with a cup of tea in hand and gasped! Jacueline quickly put her cup down and dashed towards Emily with a concerned look on her face.

'Love what it is, what has happened!'

Emily reassured her mam and asked if they could go somewhere private. Jacqueline and Emily made their way out the double doors and into the forecourt towards the seated area.

Jacqueline began,

'Now then pet, what's this all about?'

Emily proceeded with rapid speed. Jacqueline requested that she slow down and start again.

She tried once again, 'Right mam, I don't want to give up the shops completely, as you know they mean so much to me, and I have worked so hard to gain the success I have achieved'. I was thinking after the baby is born stay home for twelve months and work part time., this is where it gets tricky... I was wondering if you would look after the baby, as you said you were working towards part time at the Adult Centre next year, didn't you?'

Jaqueline sat back in her chair for a moment, and her response was a relief to Emily.

'Of course I would, my first grandchild. What about Agnes Frankie's mam? Will Frankie be alright about this? Emily looked on with a shifty look in her eyes,

'To be honest mam, I haven't asked him, I wanted to ask you first and then speak to Frankie tonight. Anyway, Agnes is not in good health with her arthritis. it would be too much for her. I am sure Frankie would be alright about it'.

Break-time was over, and they both said their goodbyes, it was settled between them. As she walked back into her classroom she was glowing with delight, and the students commented on her glowing face.

'Have you won a prize Miss; your face looks like you have won the pools or something?

Jacqueline explained that she had received excellent news and let the class know about the forthcoming birth, they were all delighted with her.

The rest of the day went smoothly for some, not so smooth for Jason at the hospital. It was noted that Jason's attire was not as impeccable as it usually is. He went into work unshaven, and his clothes looked like he had slept in them. He had; he was not himself at all.

Hazel approached him with a rather concerned look on her face. He had a look of remorse and apologized for the outburst the day before.

'Never mind about that, you look awful, what is going on with you. You need to go home and smarten yourself up. Your next patient isn't due for another ninety minutes, Go! Sort yourself out', as she pushed him out the door.

He drove home completely ashamed and disgusted in himself, he realised that he needed a good talking to, and Hazel was right, he was letting himself down. A quick bathe and change of clothes made all the difference.

As he entered the hospital car park Hazel was tentatively looking through the top floor window. Her eyes widened as she overflowed with excitement... as she quickly dashed into the lift to greet him.

Jason got out of the car and smiled at her as she approached him. 'Will I do, you were right, I did look awful'

They both made their way to the Theatre in readiness for the next patient. He was so unaware of Hazel's feelings towards him, or was he that naïve not to notice? He was certainly enjoying the attention she was giving him.

Meanwhile, Emily was rehearsing her speech with Frankie which would be in five hours' time... She sat in the back room of the haberdashery shop, repeatedly asking herself how to approach the subject of returning to work a year after the baby is born. She wasn't one for waiting, she liked to have anything in order.

The baby would be born either just before Christmas or just after... The precise date they had given her was twenty second of December.

The hours passed, it was time to venture home. As she pulled up outside the Beach House, Frankie was already home...

'Hi love, you are early', said she

'The last customer cancelled, so I thought I would get home and set the table for you. I would have cooked something simple, but you know me, I am not that good at cooking', as she smiled back at him.

'Come sit down love, I want to talk to you about something,' Oh, sounds serious pet', he looked on curiously.

'I hope you will be with me on this, but I have decided to go back to work part time when the baby is one year old. Mam said she would look after it whilst I do four hours a day. You know how much I love my work pet', as she looked towards him, hoping for a good response.'

Frankie looked back at her with an angry look on his face!

'You are kidding me right, Good Grief pet! The baby isn't born yet, and you are thinking about going back to work. What kind of a mother are you going to be, I ask myself!

Emily got up and shouted back!

'How dare you speak to me in that way! You hadn't thought it through at all have you! We would have one wage, yes, I will have some monies coming in from the ownership of the shops, but what if sales take a tumble what then! My presence at the shops! Part time, not full time! ensures sales will not! I was thinking long term! You obviously were not. You can feed yourself! I am going to Mams! She banged the front door shut!

Frankie slumped back into the armchair as the shock of it all did not register with him at all not for that moment anyway.

Emily sped away in her car towards her mam's cottage. As she pulled up, Niamh was just getting out of the car with her mam following behind her.

'Emily! What are you doing here at this time?', asked Niamh.

'I have come to have cuppa, is that alright?' said Emily with a strained look on her face.

Jacqueline followed her through the front door and sat Emily down.

'So, you have confronted Frankie with your proposal of going back to work, and it didn't go down well, did it?' said

Jacqueline, knowingly, she knew it wouldn't. Frankie is old-fashioned.

Niamh looked on confused,

'What is this? You never said anything, mam, not to me, either of you!'

Emily explained she was going to call her that very night, but it didn't go to plan. They all sat around the kitchen table. Jacqueline heated up a casserole for them all and Niamh began saying,

'Oh, Frankie will calm down sis, he loves you too much, he doesn't mean it in that way, just the heat of the moment I bet'

Emily quickly responded,

'I don't know about that sis, he looked so angry, anyway, this is what is happening, so he better get used to it'.

Niamh hadn't seen her sister that proactive! She sounded so commanding. She had a mission, and no one was going to impede her quest to succeed. Poor Frankie let's hope he does calm down.

Frankie made his way to the Fish & Chip shop along the beach, as he strolled mindfully, he hadn't noticed Father Donnelly taking his evening stroll.

'Hello young man I have not seen you on a stroll this time of the day, something on your mind lad?' he asked pensively, hoping for a good reply.

Frankie looked up at Fr Donnelly and began saying,

'I wouldn't know where to start to Father',

'Start at the beginning lad, let's just park ourselves on this bench shall we', said he.

Frankie got it all out and Fr Donnelly was eager to listen, as he smoked his pipe tentatively, his response was rather surprising to Frankie as he laid it all out...

'The way I see it lad, is it such a dilemma that the baby is taken care of by the loving Grandmother for four hours a day. You will be financially better off in the process of things so there is nothing to worry about lad, just your old-fashioned ego getting in the way. Well, that is my way of thinking on the subject. Just remember one thing: *The ties that bind us are like a woven bliss; the threads of life can get tangled up, but they don't stay tangled for long...*

Frankie was astounded, such simplicity from Fr Donnelly to make it sound absolutely alright. He got up and shook his hand with such appreciation. Father Donnelly smiled back at him with a grin of satisfaction as he said,

'Well Goodnight young Frankie, have a good evening now', as he whistled his way down the beach.

Frankie was grateful, he forgot about the Fish & Chips and quickly made his way to Jacqueline's as he ran along the beach, it was a good stretch to the Cottage, but he was in a hurry.

He eventually got there, gasping for breath as he tapped on the back door. Niamh opened it.

'My goodness Frankie, you are out of breath what have you been up to. You better come in'

Emily got up and Frankie was trying his best to get the words out, but he was still out of breath. He eventually spurted it out,

'I am sorry love, I met Fr Donnelly on the beach, and he put things right' Emily was so taken back she almost fell over but contained herself by saying, 'What on earth did Fr Donnelly say to you, I dying to know what he said'

Frankie sat down and conveyed the words of wisdom that Fr Donnelly had embarked on him. They were all so shocked, except Jacqueline, she knew Fr Donnelly was the only person to ease any burden bestowed upon him.

'Oh, what's that lovely smell', Frankie shouted out, his stomach began to rumble loudly.

Emily laughed out loud and grabbed Frankie's arm,

'It's a casserole love, and you must be starving, as we all know you cannot cook', she said sarcastically.

He kissed her passionately and whispered. 'I love you so much'

'Now, now, let's eat', said Jacqueline as she winked back at them both.

The evening ended on such a happy note, it was a blissful night for all concerned....

Chapter 4

The morning dew resonated along Sandhaven beach on this Friday morning in May, with its misty eye of promise and intrigue; what was it that refreshed the mind and soul of a sight to see as Niamh contemplated the prospect of such Ignatian... and felt very spiritual in that moment. She couldn't figure out why; it must be the calming of the sea she thought to herself....

As she sat on the window box and opened the window to feel the misty dew on her face, she began thinking of Jack. How am I going to make it up to him? She had let Jack down twice last week because of her heavy workload at Dunston School.

'I know what to do, I will book a table for two tomorrow night at his favourite bistro, 'The Signal Post', he loves it there'.

She quickly made her way downstairs to the telephone, it was 7.00am, Jack wouldn't have left for work yet. He wasn't due down the pit until 7.30am. The telephone rang for a few minutes, and Jack eventually picked it up.

As he spoke annoyingly, 'Hello!',

The reply wasn't what she had expected, Niamh never called him early in the morning. He thought it was young Sam his apprentice who worked down the pit; he was always early, and always ringing him first thing in the morning...

The conversation became a little frosty towards the end as Jack explained to Niamh, he had already made plans to go out with his mates.

A shocked Niamh went onto to say,

'No bother, no bother at all!', I haven't actually booked the table yet, have a good evening!'

Jack Slammed the telephone down,

'What a bloody cheek, let me down twice last week she thinks by clicking her fingers I will come running, well not me! as he stood talking to himself.

His mam Joan came down the stairs and asked him who he was talking to. He answered,

'Oh, just young Sam mam, I am off to pick him up, see you tonight'

He stormed out of the house, in a foul mood and sped off down the road. His day was not going well, and didn't the other pitmen get the brunt of his temper throughout the day. His closest colleague was Daniel; he took him aside at lunch time.

As they sat on the coal face with their bait tins full of spam sandwiches and a flask of tea, Daniel began saying,

'Look mate we are going out tonight with the lads, so let's have a happy face on for the rest of the day shall we...' as he patted Jack on the back.

Niamh at this time was fuming, she couldn't understand his frosty mannerism as she had explained about last week when she let him down, well, she had sort of. It was at the last minute she cancelled their two dates... It hadn't occurred to her that she was in the wrong about this.

'I am going to call our Emily, we can have a night out, after all there won't be so many of our girlie nights out after the baby is born', she said.

Emily was only too pleased to oblige her sister, as Frankie was meeting his pals to celebrate the happy news of a newly born.

As the evening progressed Emily was quite direct with Niamh and pointed out to her that she was the one that was being unreasonable. She did it in her a usual tone, she had a gift for persuading people to think like she did.

Niamh sat back in her chair sipping a glass of wine, listening away. She put the glass down and responded with Vigor.

I explained to Jack it was a busy time at school; it's the last semester. If he cannot understand how important my work is now that I am lead in the English Department then we might as well call it a day'.

Emily was shocked at her response and went on to say,

'Hold on a minute sis, you didn't give him any notice at all, that's not fair play and you know it, it's not about your work. Jack is so proud of you and has always been supportive of your work, what is going on with you sis?'

Niamh gave a concerned look back at her sister,

'I don't know sis, I just haven't got time to think about Jack right now, I am snowed under', said she.

Emily asked the question whether it was too much this promotion to Head of English, as she felt that she should balance work with a social life.

Niamh was adamant that it wasn't too much, but she needed to spend more time in meetings, and to co-ordinate the departmental strategies for the new term in September.

Once she had everything in place she would be able to breathe a little more easily. She was a forward planner, it seems she was taking it too far... too soon... there was plenty of time to plan and organize before September it was only May.

Emily was getting a little concerned, as she wanted Niamh to take a step back for a minute.

'Let's just enjoy ourselves sis, tonight anyway', as Niamh interrupted her.

The evening didn't pan out as expected, the conversation seemed to disappear after that.

'Let's call it a night shall we', said Emily.

Niamh nodded in agreement with a disappointing look on her face. They both left the bistro and flagged a taxi home. The ride home was rather quiet, even the taxi man was trying to make conversation...

Emily was dropped off first and gave her sister a rather short response. 'Bye, see you soon', with a caring look towards Niamh.

Niamh looked back at her sister and looked rather tearful, as she said goodbye.

The taxi man noted such a look and didn't make any more conversation. Niamh was relieved with that prospect; she just couldn't handle any more talk.

As she sat back in the taxi and looked out towards the sea as they drove along the Coast Road, she realized she was digging herself a hole with all this talk about work and nothing else.

She decided she would take herself off in the morning along the beachy head and have some time to herself to figure everything out.

Jack too didn't seem to have a good night either, as his pals asked why he bothered to come out at all, he was so miserable all night.

The morning came with his ray of sunshine and Niamh was happy to see it. Colm swaggered into the living room singing from the top of his voice. He was going to Bernadettes to sort out the wedding plans, and he was in such a happy mood.

He swung his arm around Niamh as she entered the room.

'Morning what a lovely morning, what are your plans on this glorious day, meeting up with Jack are you, it's a day for getting out there', he said.

Niamh smiled back at her brother and went on to say,

'I am off to beachy head bro, it's a great day for it, see you later',

She moved so fast out of the living room to avert any more questions about Jack, it wasn't the day for it.

Colm stood back,

'Well, she is in a hurry isn't she, must be love', as he muttered to himself.

Jacqueline opened the door and asked inquisitively,

'Who are you muttering to young man?'

Colm smiled back at his mam and answered,

'Our Niamh mam, you just missed her, she went out the door to Beachy End,'

'My, she is in a hurry, must be an important date or something', as Jacqueline

He looked on with a joyful look upon her face.

'Talking of important dates, I am off to Bernadette's mam, we are looking at wedding venues. I might as well tell you we are looking to get married in August,' he said.

Jacqueline grabbed her son and held him so tight he could hardly breathe.

'Oh, I am so happy son, what date have you spoken to Father Donnelly yet', as she responded eagerly.

Colm quickly replied,

'Well mam its early days yet, we just going to look at some venues for now, we haven't decided yet on a specific date, so we are holding off on that just now,' said he

'Aww I see son, well, have a fabulous day', as she hugged her son.

Colm was relieved to be walking out the door; he looked back at his mam as he got into the car and gave out a little sigh…. He hated deceiving his mam, oh how, he hoped it will all come right in the end….

Jacqueline got on with her chores and put some classical music on to dull the quietness of being home alone. She was having a moment of her own and the talk of weddings seemed to bring back thoughts of Jason.

Had she been too harsh on him lately, had she not thought this through properly. They were so well suited, and he was so caring and thoughtful towards her and her family.

She sat a while and got herself up and walked towards the telephone and before she knew it, she was dialling his number.

The telephone rang out and rang out and as she was about to put the receiver down, she heard his voice, 'Hello'.

Jacqueline stammered a moment and said, 'Hello Jason, it's Jacqueline.

'How are you? This is a lovely surprise, and what are you up to on this fine morning', as he hoped in anticipation that she would be free for the day. He just couldn't wait to see her again.

'I am just doing some chores, and I thought I would just see how you were', with a rather polite reply.

'Do you fancy a picnic along the beach today; there is a lovely little cove near you. We could sit ourselves down and have a lovely get together?' he said, hoping for a positive response.

'I think that it would be nice Jason, I know that cove it's near the rocks it's a favourite spot of mine, I will meet you there, shall we say in an hour'. She became so excited about the prospect of meeting up once again…

'I look forward to it my love', as he responded with the look of love in his eyes.

He quickly made up a basket of food; he was grateful the housekeeper had stocked his cupboards and fridge with lots of food and beverages.

As he approached the cove Jacqueline was strolling along the sand towards him, he could not get his breath. The image of Jacqueline and her slender petite figure and brown curly locks made him quiver with joy.

He greeted her with a kiss on the cheek, and they sat down on the blanket as he spread the picnic basket of food in front of her.

'You have brought enough here to feed a big family', as she laughed out loud.

Jason too laughed alongside her as he poured her a glass of wine.

It wasn't too long before the conversation reverted to his proposal of marriage.

Jacqueline spoke in a calm manner and said,

'I am not ready for such a commitment yet, I repeat yet, so can we just stay as we are for now. We have such a great relationship, isn't that enough for now', said she

He faltered at first, and began saying,

'Alright my love, I will ask you again in six months' time, is that alright with you?'.

She smiled with a wide grin on her face and kissed him firmly on the lips, 'That is a good answer, my love'

The daytime ended as they held hands walking along the sultry sandy beach barefooted....

Chapter 5

Bernadette began reflecting on her day out with Colm, as it didn't go according to plan in her eyes... She was expecting Colm to be ecstatic about the picturesque view of the Town Hall that stood back in Richmond Street.

It is a historic building with a majestic look. The old ancient architecture boldly stood out, especially the archway entrance to the Registrar office which was based at the back of the building.

It had a lovely view of a gardened forecourt, and the stain-glass windows seem to elevate the status of this old-fashioned building. It was Bernadettes ideal wedding venue.

Colm tried his best to accommodate Bernadette's enthusiasm, but he couldn't hide his disappointing eyes, as Bernadette caught many glimpses of them as they looked around the building.

It was she went home; she felt the need to have a talk with her mam.

As she arrived home and walked down the pathway, she and could hear her mam Lena calling from the back garden.

'Bernadette, come and have a look at these lovely orchids growing in their pots', she said.

Bernadette slowly made her way to the garden and looked down at the pots; she tried to smile but it didn't quite materialise. Her mam quickly noted the lack of response from her daughter.

'Well, what has happened since yesterday, I wonder?', said she.

Bernadette sat down on the garden chair adjacent to the lawn and beckoned her mam to come sit with her. She quickly accepted the invitation and Bernadette began telling her about the Town Hall and all its glory, but Colm didn't look that interested in her view.

Moreover, she went on to say that it was probably because the wedding wasn't going to be a church affair. She was so sure that Colm would be with her on this as he wasn't as religious as his mam was, is he having second thoughts? Her mind was all over the place on this bright Saturday morning.

Lena moved her hand over Bernadettes and responded in a diplomatic way.

'Marriage, my pet is a compromise, and you are sounding like this wedding is all about you when there are two people in this picture who are getting married, you need to meet him halfway. I think the pair of you need to sit down and have a good talk'

Bernadette squeezed her mam's hand and spoke gently to her,

'I keep forgetting that Dad always said you were the wise one, I do miss him mam',

'Yes, me too, I know it's been three years, but it seems like three minutes sometimes but are making the most of it aren't we. Uncle Jake is a great substitute to give you away, don't you think?', said Lena.

'You know mam, I think that's why I am opposed to having a church wedding, that walking down the aisle, it just wouldn't be the same without Dad', said Bernadette'.

Lena glanced at her daughter and gave her thoughtful look before saying, 'I thought as much pet, you should talk to Colm about this, soon',

They sat in the garden and decided to have breakfast outside as it wasn't that cold for a May Spring morning, as the sun was so refreshing on the skin. It elevated Bernadette's mood. She would call him right away as she didn't want to waste any time.

As she made her way into the hallway, the telephone rang out, it was Colm on the other line, he had beat her to it.

She spoke first in a joyful tone of voice,

'Hi sweetheart, I was just about to call you, how telepathic you' are, we are in sync with one another',

'Well, I do hope so pet saying that we are about to get married, it's a good thing don't you think', as he laughed down the telephone.

She quickly went on to say,

'I need to talk to you about the wedding, pick me up in five minutes and we can go down to the beach café, Carries', her voice started to quake a little.

'Alright pet, on my way', he replied.

Colm was getting excited about the prospect of his fiancé having made a definite decision about where and when they were getting married, as it was just sitting there without any dates settled.

As they drove to the café, Colm began asking about that very thing.

'Let's just wait until we are there and we can have a good talk about it', said she.

They made their way to the tables which were set out near the beach front with its pebbled stones that were embedded across the sandy beach. There were mounted stone tubs that had an arrangement of planted flowers in them, which consisted of daises, daffodils, and tulips. The tubs were carefully assembled alongside the café.

As they sat with their coffees and muffins, Bernadette paused and then revealed all. She wanted Colm to understand why she wasn't confident about a church wedding.

Colm replied in his caring manner,

'It's alright pet, if you want to get married in the Town Hall, then that's fine by me, I want you to be happy'.

'It's your day too love, it's just you didn't seem that enthusiastic about the Town Hall. You seem to saunter through the process, was it because it didn't look anything like a church… I know you. I could tell by the expression on your face,' as she gave him a firm look.

'Oh, it was that obvious was it, oops, dad used to tell me about that, my eyes are a true giveaway', as he gave out a wry smile.

Colm was ready for a good compromise, and he was very good at problem solving it was part of his job in the draughtsman's office. He quickly relayed his thoughts to Bernadette.

'I tell you what, why don't we have the wedding at the Town Hall, and we could ask Father Donnelly to bless our wedding afterwards down on the beach, he loved his strolls along the beach, I don't think it would be too much of an imposition to him, what you think then', as he waiting for Bernadettes reply…

Bernadette looked so surprised it wasn't what she had expected but she was more than happy with this outcome, as it meant everyone would be happy with that, especially Jacqueline.

Colm looked relieved, and spoke out with confidence in his voice…

'Right, we better get across to the Town Hall and get this booked and we might as well take a look at Stable wood Hall, just down the road from the Town Hall',

'I never thought of the Hall, is it nice inside', said she

'It is, it is not very big, but you said you didn't want anything big, I went to the Christmas Office Party there last year, I think you would like it'.

Bernadette was getting enthusiastic about the whole idea of getting the wedding sorted today and the reception.

As they made their way to the hall, Bernadette was taken back by the two seahorses mounted in grey slated stone that stood side by side on the entrance steps. It was owned by a family who bred horses from Chilsford, on an estate set back just passed Alnwick.

Its interior was rather like a farmhouse than a hall, with its beaded rafters and leather sequences littered around the crevices in each corner. It had a cosy welcoming feel about it and Bernadette was feeling the effect of that.

She grabbed Colm's hand and squeezed it,

'This is for us, this is definitely for us, I hope they are not booked on our special day', as she spoke with a hopeful tone in her voice.

They made their way to the reception desk and nervously waited for the manager to arrive to give them hopefully good news.

Mr Andersby a tall light-haired man walked confidently towards them. He was impeccably dressed in his navy-blue suit and tie. His white shirt with a stiff collar that looked like it had been starched for hours...

He spoke so eloquently, as he outlined what was on offer when booking their wedding package. He directly opened the diary to check the availability as he did so,

Colm crossed his fingers...

'Ah! you are in luck, we don't have definite booking but there are some pending so if you want to make a firm booking then a deposit of £25 would have to be paid today', he said directly.

Bernadette turned to Colm and he responded,

'We can do this, the building society is open until 1pm, it's noon, so I will leave you here with Mr Andersby and be back in ten minutes, don't go anywhere', as he rushed out of the door.

Mr Andersby escorted Bernadette to the wedding venue which was located through the double doors and up the very polished Mahogony wooden staircase, she could see her reflection through the Bannister as she mounted the twelve steps.

As he opened the door for Bernadette, she looked amazed, as she studied the archways with their flowered effect in each alcove there were tables of six and at the front there was a large banquet table for the bride and groom and family.

'Is this to your liking Bernadette, may I call you Bernadette', as he asked politely.

'Of course you can, it is very much to my liking, it's so warm and friendly, I love it'.

Colm arrived back and the receptionist guided him towards the wedding venue, he stood back and shouted,

'Wow, this isn't like it was when I came to the Christmas Party, this is much better', as he looked around the room in amazement.

Mr Andersby spoke up,

'Oh, you have been here before, well, we go all out for wedding venues, and we do have complimentary champagne on arrival; the owners have always done this'.

They all made their way to Mr Andersby's office to pay the deposit, Colm was nifty a saver, he kept his monies in the building society. He had inherited his father's way of 'spend what you need to and save the rest'. He smiled at Mr Andersby as he handed over the monies. It was at that moment he felt the presence of his late father near hand, it was a nice moment, but it quickly subsided.

Bernadette and Colm went on to discuss the menu. The buffet seemed to catch their eye as there were more than enough different delicacies available, and everyone could just help themselves.

The sit-down meal was rather lavish and expensive, and Bernadette was adamant that the buffet would be adequate for their needs. She was like Colm in that way, a saver, as she didn't like to squander her money. They had so much in common.

She would decide the colour of the sashes that were to be arranged around the chairs later as she didn't know what wedding dress she was wearing yet. It was going to be a simple wedding dress; she just hadn't found that simplicity yet.

They discussed the time frame as their wedding at the Town Hall was booked for 1.00pm

Mr Andersby informed them that the venue would be ready as soon as they arrived. The day was going so well as they practically skipped their way to the car.

Colm was overcome with excitement,

'Let's go and tell everyone, your mam first, then my mam, and then Uncle Dylan'.

Bernadette's mam was overcome with joy as she kissed them both on their arrival.

As they made their way to Jacqueline's Colm parked the car outside and took a deep breath, Bernadette noticed his anguish…

'Oh, my, what a surprise, I thought you were out for the day', as Jacqueline spoke.

'We have come to tell you something mam, that we have booked the wedding and the venue, and we wanted you to know as we have just told Bernadette's mam. We are getting married at the Town Hall and having the reception at Stable Wood Hall'.

Jacqueline couldn't believe it, she tried to hide the disappointment in her eyes as she looked at Colm, and he quickly responded,

'Oh, yes, we are going to ask Father Donnelly if we can have the marriage bless down on the beach afterwards, I hope he will'.

Jacqueline moved towards him and hugged him so tightly and said, 'I am sure he will, I am so happy for you two, I really am'.

She then went to Bernadette and gave her a hug and kiss on the cheek. Bernadette looked to Colm, and they all hugged together... ....

Chapter 6

Jacqueline couldn't contain her joy and excitement of the forthcoming wedding of her son. She was so happy to see two of her children settled, but it was Niamh she was concerned about now.

'I must talk to her properly on the way home from the college, I will suggest we have tea out for a change', as she muttered to herself.

Niamh was pre-occupied as she dropped her mam off at the car park to the Adult Centre. Jacqueline grabbed her hand,

'Before you rush off love, I have booked a table for us at the Castle Inn, it's my treat', she was anticipating a warm reply.

Niamh looked towards her mam,

'Why mam, what's this about, do you have some news, I don't know about', she asked curiously.

Jacqueline made a sly gesture,

'Something like that, see you at 4.30pm, as she replied coyly...

There was no way she going to get into a conversation about it, she wanted to see if she could mediate a little between her daughter and Jack. She knew how stubborn her Niamh could get; she had inherited that from her...

Emily had pointed out to her that Niamh was doing far too much at work and she was worried she was going to burn herself out. Jacqueline was hoping a mother's touch might help.

The day went over rather quickly, and Niamh looked a little irritated as she picked her mam up, as she wanted to stay on at work to go through the teaching plans which were in fact already set out...

They arrived at the Castle Inn, and Niamh was feeling rather peckish, as she wasn't eating lunch these days..., it seemed to be the norm with her. Jacqueline couldn't help but notice that Niamh looked like she was losing weight...

'The salmon pasta dish looks right up your street pet', said Jacqueline

'Yes, I will have that mam thanks', she replied with no thought at all to what she was replying to.

Jacqueline went for her usual catch of the day, a good-sized haddock with Chips and mushy peas. Niamh laughed out loud and said,

'I don't know where you put the food, mam but you never put weight on'.

Jacqueline quickly responded,

'You look like you could do with a few pounds on lass'

'I know mam, I have been nitpicking at my lunches, yes, I will sort myself out, don't worry mam.

Anyway, changing the subject, what is it you wanted to talk about. I know you want to talk about something, as you wouldn't have suggested tea out, would you?' said she.

Jacqueline, put her glass of wine down and went on to say,

'I am worried about you, I notice Jack hasn't been around for a while, is everything alright with you two? All you talk about is your students and teaching plans these days love, you need to separate yourself from it and have a social life pet'.

Niamh banged her glass down and got out of her chair and made her way to the ladies. Jacqueline sat for a moment and left her on her own to calm down. It was some minutes before she returned to and hurriedly picked her bag up and said rather snipingly...

'I have lost my appetite, you can make your way home,'

Jacqueline was stunned by Niamh's character she had never seen her like this; it was more concerning than she thought. This new promotion was destroying her, and she couldn't see it.

She stayed at the restaurant and ate her food slowly as she tried to come to terms with Niamh's sudden outburst.

Suddenly she noticed other customers making their way to the window overlooking the car park.

'Oh! my goodness! Something has happened in the car park, there are policemen and a policewoman out there; an ambulance has just pulled up', shouted one of the spectators.

Jacqueline quickly got out of her chair and noticed a commotion; it seemed to be in the direction of Niamh's car. She rushed out of the restaurant and saw Niamh lying on the ground. There was blood everywhere.

'Oh! my bairn, my bairn, who has done this!' Jacqueline cried out.

The policewoman guided Jacqueline away for a moment and conveyed to her what had happened. Two skinheads had attacked Niamh and took her bag; There were two witnesses who saw the incident.

The policeman took statements from them both and thanked them for acting so quickly to the incident.

Jacqueline became distraught and was escorted towards the ambulance.

The paramedics explained that they didn't know the full extent of Niamh's injuries, and it was best to wait until they got to the hospital, and the experts could have a look at her. They would keep her stabilised for now.

When they arrived, Hazel, Jason's assistant, was there to meet the paramedics. She explained that Mr Sampson was on call, and he would be dealing with Niamh. As Hazel glanced at Jacqueline, she then realised who she was.

'Jason isn't on call, he won't be here until tomorrow, it will be Mr Sampson who will take care of Niamh', as she stood back rather proud of her response...

'Can you call Jason please, I would like him to know that I am here with Niamh', Jacqueline spoke in a tender voice.

'I am sorry Jacqueline, but it is not protocol as Mr Sampson is the Consultant under Niamh's care as he is the one on call and Jason is not, she replied rather abruptly.

Jacqueline quickly turned away from her and proceeded towards Niamh.

'You need to wait in the waiting room, Mr Sampson will call you when he has finished his assessment,'

Jacqueline gave her a deadly stare and walked away. She made her way to the telephone booth to call Emily and Colm.

They both arrived promptly together, Colm called Jack before heading out and he wasn't far behind them.

'It's a waiting game, we must just wait on Mr Sampson to come to us', said Jacqueline.

'How did this happen?' said Colm

'I don't know we were in the restaurant, and we had a little tiff... she stormed out! All I know is that two skin heads mugged and attacked her...Jacqueline said tearfully...

Jack was distraught,

'I feel so guilty, the last time we spoke which was days ago, I was not pleased with her at all with all this talk of work... I wish I had understood her better',

Colm patted him on the shoulder,

'She will be fine, our Niamh, tough as old boots', he said in a confident manner.

Mr Sampson made his way into the waiting room and began staying,

'She has a nasty gash on her head, but the scan has come back with no prominent damage. She has a few cracked ribs. We will keep her in for a few days to observe. There could be psychological damage given the ferocity of the attack. I would suggest she seeks medical advice; a counsellor may help in that field. I can arrange that if you wish'.

Jacqueline gave out a sigh of relief as all of them did, as they sat together. 'Can I see her; can I see her!' shouted Jack

Mr Sampson conveyed the news to them all that she had been given a sedative, as she was totally traumatised, and it would be a few hours before she was awake. He suggested they go for a coffee and come back later. Colm spoke first,

'I should call Uncle Dylan, you know how close he is to our Niamh'

Yes, that's a good idea son', Jacqueline replied.

Dylan arrived within the hour, and it was time for them to go and see Niamh. As she awoke, she screamed out,

'Get off me, get off me!'.

Jacqueline quickly went to her bedside,

'It's mam, sweetheart, you are alright pet, calm yourself now'.

She breathed heavily, still shaking, as Jack approached.

'Oh, my love, you just rest now, everything is going to be alright'.

Niamh calmed herself a little and held his hand, she smiled bravely and was glad he was by her side.

That feeling came upon her, it was if she was reliving the attempted rape attack when she was at university.

The only thing that comforted her was that she was brave and attempted to see the assailants off. She wasn't that weak girl anymore…

Emily sat at the other side of the bed and Niamh attempted to turn herself towards her put yelled out with pain!

'Don't move our Niamh, I will come round to you, as Jacqueline moved out of the way.

They both held each other, and Emily couldn't contain herself as she wept out loudly.

Mr Sampson intervened and said it was time for Niamh to get some rest.

As they left the hospital, Hazel was standing in the corridor and gave Jaqueline a rather spiteful look… She had no intention of calling Jason, he was her love not Jacqueline's… she was fixed on the process of having Jason for herself and would go all out to obtain his affection….

Jacqueline arrived home exhausted, as she went to put the kettle on for her and Colm, he turned to his mam and spoke out,

'You should call Jason mam; I am sure he would like to know what's happened'

'Yes, you are right son, I will go and do that, you pour the tea son', as she made her way to the telephone table.

As the telephone rang out for a moment, Jason came dashing down the stairs to answer it.

'Hello!', he said loudly.

'Well, hello you', Jacqueline answered.

A long paused proceeded and it was Jason who softly said, 'It's lovely to hear from you, how are you?'

She took her time and eventually replied, it had been a week since they last spoke.

Jacqueline didn't hold back and quickly outlined the events of that night to him and he became rather angry with his assistant, he felt she could have made the effort, knowing that he was a close friend of the family. He would be having a quick word with her in the morning.

He reassured Jacqueline that he would take over the care of Niamh, as Mr Sampson was a locum and wasn't permanently residing at that hospital as he would be moving around.

The next day, Jason confronted Hazel, and she denied that she was asked to make such a call. She quickly went on to say it was rush- time in the hospital, so many arrivals, and she couldn't recall such a request.

He then quietened down somewhat, and they went about their daily business, as Hazel gave him his usual coffee and loving smile, which he never acknowledged.

She was determined to win him around at any cost...

Chapter 7

Niamh began rustling the sheets back and forth she couldn't settle in this hospital bed, she was going home tomorrow, and she wouldn't take 'no' for an answer.

'To pot with this, I am going home no matter what the Doctor says', she muttered to herself at 3am in the morning.

She managed to get a few hours' sleep. It was the clatter of cups and saucers that woke Niamh, as the auxiliary nurse came by with a trolley full and tea and coffee, it was 7.30am time for the early cuppa.

'Tea or coffee', she asked Niamh with a friendly smile on her face.

Niamh sat up and asked for her coffee, she needed it to stay awake as she was going home in her mind. Her head was a little sore and her ribs, but she could make it to the toilet on her own and she was happy with that.

She turned to the staff nurse on duty and asked if there would be a possibility of her returning home given that she can now go to the toilet unaided.

'I will let the Doctor know Niamh, he is the expert, but it's a good sign if you have a competent gait and your visuals are good. He will check for himself', as she spoke with confidence.

'Competent gait? What is that when it's at home', asked Niamh.

'It your competence in walking, gait just means the way you walk', she replied 'Well, I never, I teach literature, but I haven't come across that one?' Niamh was bemused at this newfound word of explanation.

'It's just one of those medical terms you come across in medicine', said she. 'I will make a note of that one', Niamh laughed out loud.

Jason briskly walked into the ward and made his way to Niamh's bed. 'Good morning, Niamh, how are you this fine morning'.

'I am feeling rather good Doctor, I have been to the toilet unaided, and my gait is excellent', as she winked at Nurse Catherine.

Jason smiled widely back at her,

'Well, let's have a look at you shall we. Your head is healing nicely, so, let's just have a look at these ribs shall we',

Niamh winched and clasped her lips tightly…it hurt, but she wasn't going to let him know how much it hurt, she wanted to get home today!

'Mmm, these ribs will take a few weeks to heal, but I think you could do your convalescence at home Niamh, and you can come back and see me in a few weeks to get checked over, how does that sound to you', he asked.

'Music to my ears Doctor', as she grinned back at him like a Chesire Cat.

'I thought as much, your bed is your kingdom, and these hospital beds are not the best', as he whispered to Niamh. It wasn't exactly hospital protocol to let out that kind of information. She smiled back at him, and shook his hand,

'Thank you so much',

As Jason turned to walk towards another patient, Jacqueline appeared, she walked quickly towards him.

'How is my Niamh', she asked earnestly.

He held Jacqueline's arm and responded,

'You will be pleased to know, you can take her home, she needs to rest completely for at least two weeks so the ribs can heal. I will see her back here in two weeks, or I could just call round in a few days to see how everyone is doing',

'Oh, that is fabulous news Jason, and you can call round anytime you know that', said she, with a caring look towards him.

Jason was elevated with excitement, he would call the very next day, he couldn't wait to see Jacqueline.

Jacqueline made her way to Niamh' s bed and put her arms around her daughter,

'I cannot wait to get you home and settled, I have been worried out of my mind',

Niamh looked wearily at her mam and spoke in a pleading tone...

'Me too mam, I just want to get out of here, I am so sorry mam, talking in that horrible way to you in the restaurant, I will never ever do that again, I just lost it, I am not going to let the job take over my life, not anymore, I am going to ask to either step down or they give me an assistant, I have been thinking about it all night',

Jacqueline was so pleased to hear that as she kissed her daughter on the cheek.

'Let's get you dressed, do you need a hand, or shall I just leave you for a minute,

'I can manage mam, see you in a min',

Jacqueline pulled the curtains around Niamh and sat in the chair adjacent. Hazel, Jason's assistant, just happened to walk into the ward and gave Jacqueline a rather sly look as she hurriedly made her way to Jason's side. She deliberately put her arm on his shoulder, so Jacqueline had full view of this.

'What are doing? Why are you on the ward, as he shrugged her hand away from him.

Hazel took a step back, rather stunned by his reaction, and went on to say,

'There is a phone call from the lab, I thought you would want to take it', said she 'I will be along presently', just ask them to hold on, he answered abruptly.

Before he made his way to the office, he went over to say goodbye to Jacqueline and Niamh. He took Jacqueline aside for a moment in the corridor and said,

'I will see you tomorrow at 7pm.'

Jacqueline quickly replied with 'Yes, look forward to it'.

As they lingered together for moment, Hazel caught sight of their closeness and snared at them both as she walked into the office and banged the stapler up and down on his desk.

'I won't have this, she is not having him, if I cannot have him, then nobody is having him'…

As she turned to walk out of the office Jason appeared, and she quickly told him that she was needed on the ward. He couldn't help but notice how flushed her face was. He hoped he hadn't offended her with his manner earlier.

Dylan had arrived to pick Niamh and Jacqueline up before he made his way to the Shipyard, he had left his colleague Jim, a competent engineer on the ship to hold the fort for a few hours, the ship was drydocked so it wasn't going anywhere, as the repairs would take some days to fix. He had a few hours to spend with his favourite niece.

Niamh was so happy to see him, as she asked about Serena and the twins.

'I am off work for a few weeks Uncle Dylan, so I hope to see those beautiful babies when I am up and about properly',

'We will all come over on Saturday, how does that sound', as he gave her cheeky wink.

Niamh smiled back at her uncle and spoke 'That would be fantastic!'

Niamh was feeling better by the minute, she needed to put things right with Jack, she felt so guilty about how she had treated him these past weeks. She would call him that night as he was due home from the pit side at.6.30pm.

They all arrived at the cottage and Jacqueline took Niamh's arm and guided her to sofa. She was nicely settled with a blanket around her. Jacqueline swiftly went into the kitchen to make lunch for them all.

Dylan began telling Niamh all about Amy and Ethan, they were crawling now, but Amy was the instigator. She was the one that wanted to get a head start on Ethan and he quickly responded to her competitive streak. She looked like she was going to be the bossy one.

Niamh listened with excitement in her eyes.

'I bet they will be walking soon, I bet, said she.

Dylan agreed by saying,

'You might be right, but my money is on Amy to get mounted first along the sofa. She has been trying to pull herself up when she is near the sofa but plops down on her backside. I have no doubt she will keep trying'.

Lunch was ready, it was a light lunch, ham and salad, as Niamh didn't want anything heavy not with those ribs...

Jacqueline enquired about Serena and asked how she was finding being at home all day. Dylan responded by saying,

'She is loving it being with her babies. She was knitting away and making some lovely cross stitch portraits for Emily's gallery.

Furthermore, Dylan went on to say that he wondered if Serena would ever return to her father's law firm, not for a few years at least.

Jacqueline and Niamh were not surprised as they both felt that Serena was a natural mother, and she took to the learnings of knitting and cross stitch so rapidly. Emily was a great teacher.

They all had lovely afternoon together and Jacqueline demanded that Niamh go up to bed to get some rest. She was more than happy to do that as she was so tired, she would sleep until the next day, she felt in her mind.

It was Colm, who woke her up the next morning, it was 7am; she couldn't mistake his clumping foot prints up the stairs. He made such a clatter as he entered her bedroom

'Hey sis, good to see you, as he kissed her on the cheek.

'Well, I am awake now, you made sure of that', she laughed out loudly. 'Oh, you're asleep then', as he slyly gives her a cheeky wink.

She couldn't be mad with her lovely cheeky brother, as she smiled back at him.

'Do me a favour Colm, give Jack a call and tell him I am home, I was going to ring him, but I have been asleep all afternoon', she asked nicely.

'I already called him this morning sis, told him you were coming home, Mam called me at the office earlier'. He will be around in about half an hour.

'Oh! My goodness, look at the state of me, he cannot see me like this, keep him downstairs will you', she says pleading with her brother.

'Alright sis, you look alright to me', as he stood smirking away at her dishevelled hair.

'Oh' Shush, you always say that, go on with you, go! Now go! as she tried to push him off the bed, but her ribs were hurting now. She quickly took some painkillers by the side of her bed.

She made her way to the bathroom, brushed her teeth, washed her face, and combed her hair. As she looked in the mirror, she decided to put a little makeup on as she looked rather pale.

I will put my new PJs on they are rather fetching as she looked in the full-length mirror in her bedroom; she laughed at herself and got back into bed with her book of poetry, Emily Dickinson... The author had such a gift of embracing life and the joy of it.

The doorbell rang out; Niamh quickly sat up and ran her fingers through her brown hair. She felt the fluttering in her stomach as the door opened and in walked Jack with a bouquet of twelve red roses and box of milk tray chocolates.

'Oh my, Jack, that is so lovely of you, they are so lovely', as she smelt the roses

Jack sat at her bedside and moved towards her and kissed her on the lips. She responded effectively to Jack's surprise. The kiss lingered a while and as they broke away from one another Niamh began to say,

'I am so sorry love, I have been an absolute nightmare these passed weeks, I love you, I really do'.

Jack stood powerless, he was ecstatic at such a statement. He bent forwards and put his hands around Niamh's face,

'I love you more, my beautiful Niamh, I couldn't love anyone as much as I love you'.

They hugged, but Jack hugged too hard, and Niamh winched out, 'Ouch! Niamh screamed out, these flipping ribs!

'Oh! Love I am so sorry, as he moved back, I wouldn't hurt you for the world', 'You better not, as we are going to be together forever',

Jack's mind at that point was spinning, he had the engagement ring in his pocket, it had been there for weeks. He was going to ask her to marry him just before the first row they had a few weeks back. He quickly got off the bed and went down on one knee and said,

'My beautiful Niamh, this ring has been burning a hole in my pocket for weeks now, so please put me out of my misery and marry me, I love you so much',

She paused for a moment as Jack eagerly awaiting her reply.

'I do, I do, I will, I will', she said out loud over, and over... They both lay on the bed with tears in their eyes....

Chapter 8

There was a sprinkle of a summer fragrance in the air on this first day of June, its powerful essence lingered in the air, as the warm breeze filtered through the open windows.

'Summertime the season of light... Its fragrance so vibrant so bright...

The sunlight beckons on the sandy beach... The joy of a restful release...

Jacqueline couldn't help herself; she wrote down her poetic feelings of summer this bright Saturday morning. She was inspired with utmost joy, her Niamh was now settled, and she couldn't be happier, she was bursting.

She quickly got up from her garden chair and didn't realise she had been sitting in the garden for over an hour; it was a beautiful view; the sunlit sky and its glorified zoom across the sea and sand....

June, she couldn't believe how the months had passed by, suddenly it came to her. A family gathering to celebrate all our happy news. After all there are two weddings coming up, Colm and Niamh and Emily with the forthcoming baby, let's not forget that.

Dylan, Serena and baby are coming this afternoon, she said to herself.

'I will call our Aileen and Sara to complete the family gathering. I will call Jason too. It wouldn't be complete without him'. She was falling in love again and she knew it.

Niamh was feeling a little stiff as she got out of her bed, but as soon as she looked out of the window and saw the beautiful sun lighting up the sky, she soon forgot about her stiffness. There was too much happiness in her heart she felt like she too would burst.

Jacqueline shouted to Colm as he came down the stairs,

'It was time to get the family together; she shouted to Colm who was pleased to hear about the family get-together. She then made her way up the stairs to see how Niamh was doing.

This announcement had cheered up Niamh as she brightly responded,

'Oh! what a good idea mam on this beautiful day of sunshine, as she sat up in her bedside chair rather spritely.

'Alright pet, now I don't want you doing anything but to get yourself bathed and clothed and you are to sit in the garden. I have put you in the chair that extends so you can put your feet up, and that's an order', said Jacqueline in her firm manner.

'Right Oh Mam, you are the boss', as Niamh saluted her mam with a wry smile and slight wink at her.

'Colm, I need you to take me to the shops pronto, as no time to lose lots to do', 'No bother mam, be with you in a tick',

Jacqueline went straight to the butchers to buy some steaks, sausages, chicken, and joint of gammon. She proceeded to the Co-op to buy flour, butter, castor sugar, vanilla essence, and finger sponges, chocolate and cream. Then to the bakers for fresh bread and buns. She was in the mood for baking, biscuits, cakes and trifles.

'Wow mam, you are going all out today aren't you', said Colm licking his lips. 'I certainly am lad, it's a big day for celebrations', she said energetically.

As time went by, everyone arrived at 3pm, Colm and Bernadette had assisted Jacqueline in preparing the outside table and chairs, they had spare chairs in the brick built shed alongside the wooden shed.

Jacqueline managed to create some chocolate biscuits, a Victoria Sponge cake and two chocolate trifles. There were various selections on sandwiches and cooked meats and if the boys fancied their burgers, Dylan could accommodate, he was great at cooking burgers and steaks on the grill. That was Declan and Dylan's favourite past time in the summer.

Jason, however, was delayed, he was on call this weekend. He received a call from the hospital saying there was an emergency. As entered the hospital and made his way to the emergency pre assessment wing where the emergency was seemingly taking place. That was not the case as the senior registrar looked confused.

'I not sure where the call came from, but it wasn't from our wing, maybe the operative made a mistake?'

'Everything alright otherwise', Jason asked

'Yes, we are doing fine, if there is problem, I will page you personally',

He waved back at the registrar as he left the department, he walked down the corridor and who should he bump into but Hazel. She greeted him with a warm smile.

'Hello Jason fancy seeing you here',

'Yes, well, it was a false alarm, someone paged me to say there was an emergency. It turned out not to be', as he looked rather annoyed at the fact he had to make the journey.

'You are here now, so why don't we go for some lunch', hoping for a positive response.

'I have to dash, I'm expected at Jacqueline's, a family party',

'Oh, but you are not family', 'Well, I hope to be very soon',

Hazel clasped her lips tightly to avoid her utter contempt at such a response. She had instigated the call as she sneaked into the pre-assessment ward. The senior registrar had left his pager on the desk as he was seeing to a patient and she couldn't let this idea slip away, she wanted Jason there with her for lunch.

'I will see you on Monday Hazel, have a good weekend', he spoke directly to her with a half-hearted look on his face.

'Bye for now', she said as she held herself together and quickly made her way to the office and slammed the door loudly …

'I will get you in the end, mark my words', as she sat planning her next move…

Jason made his way home and quickly changed into a fresh polo shirt and he decided to put his chino trousers on as it was so warm.

Everyone had arrived. Niamh was so happy to see the twins as they crawled across the quilted blankets on the grass, they were happy to just explore their new surroundings. Serena was on the go every five minutes with them both. Dylan went to the car and brought out the play pen so she could have five minutes' peace.

Jason had eventually arrived and made his way to Niamh to check on his patient. He was more than happy to see her looking well.

Dylan shouted over to Jason,

'Hey Jason, come give us hand with the grilling mate,'
'I will be with you in a tick mate',

He conveyed his delight to Niamh and told her not to overdo it this week.

His assistance was needed, and he quickly made his way to Dylan. He got right into it as he grilled more sausages, steaks and burgers.

Dylan stood back with admiration and spoke 'You're a natural at this Jason',

My sister has me around for barbecues all the time, she insists. I always oblige, as he winked back at Dylan.

Jacqueline looked over to them both, she felt a feeling of comfort as if Declan was saying to her, 'it's alright love, I approve'.

She went over to them both and said,

'Don't you burn them mind, I like mine done but not burnt to a crisp'. As she put her arm around Jason's waist; he was loving it.

Emily was famished; she was always hungry, being almost five months now.

'You best give Emily the large plate Jacqueline, she has been eating for two now', said Frank smiling away.

Emily was blossoming like a fine rose, and she was watching the twins tentatively thinking, 'this will be me soon', the anticipation and excitement overwhelmed her at times, but it was such a lovely feeling.

She sat long aside Serena who pointed out to her that it wouldn't be long before she felt the baby kicking. Emily explained to her that she had experienced what she called 'fluttering's' but thought it was just her being overwhelmed.

She was eager to know more from Serena, as they sat together most of the afternoon. It was so refreshing and a relief to have someone so nearby who can give her this sound advice she thought to herself.

Jacqueline spent a lot of time with her sisters as they were eager to know how things are going with Jason. They were both so happy to hear such good news.

'You are absolutely beaming sis, glowing in fact', said Sara

'It's the sun, get away with you', Jacqueline laughed off such a notion.

'I have to admit our Jacqueline, our Sara is right, and you know it', Aileen answered back.

'Oh, alright then, yes, I have fallen in love with him, I didn't think this would happen. I love Declan still, always will, but today, I felt him give me that approval. I cannot explain it, but it was there', as Jacqueline spoke with such adoration.

Aileen and Sara looked at one another bemused, but went onto say, 'That's a good thing isn't it',

The three sat and sipped their glass of wine and made a toast for the future 'To the Gibsons, may the joy happiness linger on and on'. 'Cheers to that', as they all stood up.

Jason and Dylan made their way to the girls,

'What's this about then, what's going on here'.

'That's for us to know and for you two to find out', as Sara, put her finger on her nose… and tapped it, indicating that you won't get to know…

'We are off to get some more beers, we will leave you to your secrets', said Dylan.

Niamh and Jack sat together all through the afternoon, the only time Jack left her side was for food and drink. They were besotted as they talked about their plans.

Niamh would like a church wedding, and her Uncle Dylan would take her down the aisle. They just couldn't decide when that would be, as they didn't want to spoil Colm's and Bernadette's day. It was settled they would leave it for a while at least.

The sun began to go down, and it was time to pack up. They all made their way inside.

'Shall we play the game, Charades', Colm spoke out.

Jacqueline quickly responded by saying,

'What a good idea, I will get the cards,'

She went to the drawer to collect them. The cards were made by Declan many years ago, so Jacqueline knew all of them. Colm and Niamh were the best players. Jacqueline was intrigued to see if Jason would guess the right answers. It turned out he was better than any of them. The game went on for an hour or so.

The twins were tired out and so was Serena. Emily was feeling a little tired herself, and Niamh was exhausted.

Jack took her to her bed and stayed with her until she fell asleep.

Colm took Bernadette home and the house was left with Jason and Jacqueline as they embraced in the garden. They both decided to take a walk along the beach.

'This has been the best day of my life sweetheart', said Jason.

'I am happy to hear that because it's one of mine too', as she went on further to say,

'We have two marriages coming up love, so we will just have to bide our time and let the young ones have their day. Our day will come thereafter, soon thereafter, she said with conviction…

Jason was so warmed with that gesture, he was in complete agreement and kissed Jacqueline so passionately, he almost took her breath away…

The evening was over, and the weekend would end with love all around.

'So much happiness, I hope it lasts ', Jacqueline mutter to herself as she fell asleep

Chapter 9

The next few months went along quite smoothly, with exception of Hazel and her endeavours to gain Jason's affection. He just couldn't see through her as he was blindsided with his love for Jacqueline and her family.

Her inadvertent innuendos towards Jason of having tickets for an opera at the weekend didn't seem to register with him. She thought she would get a good response from him, as she knew how he loved classical music.

As they made their way down the corridor and into the lift to the operating theatres. Jason held the lift open and in walked Emily and Frank, they were on their way to the maternity ward for the usual check-up.

Jason was elated and greeted them both with such familiarity and warmth. Hazel stood back in anger. Her thoughts were becoming sinister towards Jason; this obsession she had developed towards him was getting out of control!

Emily was feeling her baby kick now and she was looking so radiant, and she couldn't help but portray such feelings of joy as she spoke,

'My baby is now kicking, it's such a wonderful Jason, I cannot believe it, it takes my breath away'.

Jason replied with such a caring manner,

'You will feel the baby more as it goes along and I am sure it will be a fine- looking baby just like it's mam and dad'

She further continued the conversation and went on to say,

'I am preparing for Bernadette's handmade wedding dress; I will be making it for her.

Jason became nostalgic at that moment, thinking about when he proposed to Jacqueline. He quickly reverted to Emily and went onto say,

'Don't tire yourself out too much young lady, just take it easy' Emily smiled back with her reply,

'I won't do that Jason; Frankie will be there keeping a close eye on me'.

As Frankie and Emily drove back home from the hospital Emily recalled the conversation with Bernadette and how everything had come to a head... It was when Bernadette's mam decided to step in and pay for an expensive dress. This wasn't going to happen and Bernadette made sure of that. She approached Emily as she knew how gifted she was with stitching. The haberdashery shop had such a selection of silks and cotton fabrics.

A few weeks prior, after having had an awful row with her mam, she took herself off along the coast road, and when she stopped at the embankment there was Emily's shop which stood proudly on the corner side. It was that moment when she saw the fabrics in the window, she would approach Emily, and she agreed heart-heartedly.

Emily dug out several patterns, and it was the third pattern that stood out for Bernadette it was simple streamline dress with consisted of sophisticated high neck which would have lace effect stitched upon the satin material.

It would be full length without a trail, and Emily suggested bringing the fabric in line with the boat neckline. She would place lace around the neckline, cuffs, and around the waistline to bring the dress alive, and it wouldn't be too plain.

Bernadette was so happy about the outcome as she had picked out a laced half-moon head piece which she found more fitting for her rather than a long veil.

The cost was to Bernadette's liking, but Emily had other plans. She wanted it to be a wedding gift, and she got her way. As she went on to say,

'It's our Colm you are marrying so you cannot say no to that, can you?' Bernadette hugged Emily with a delightful look on her face.

She proceeded home to let her mam know about the dress and it was to Lena's liking.

It was now time to approach Father Donnelly as Colm drove up the drive to pick Emily up. Her mam answered the door and greeted Colm with loving gesture, and went on to say,

'I hope everything works out tonight with the priest, as I know it means a lot to you Colm; and Bernadette is with you on this I know'.

Colm answered in his usual laid back tone,

'Everything is fine Lena; don't you worry about anything'.

As they arrived at the Presbytery, Father Donnelly came out to greet them in his usual lively manner

'Well, hello you two, and what do I owe this pleasure'.

As Colm moved forward, he began to say,

'We both need a favour from you Father'.

Father Donnelly looked intrigued

'You best come in, and I will pop the kettle on and there will be ginger nut biscuits to snack on. You cannot have a cup of tea without a biscuit'. He was partial to his tea and biscuits; he called it his daily ritual.

As they sat in the rather large kitchen with his large oak table and chairs and sipped their tea and crunched a biscuit Colm began,

'It's like this Father; Bernadette isn't a Catholic and would like to have our wedding service at the Town Hall. We both thought it would be a good idea to ask your permission to bless our wedding vows on the beach thereafter. If that's not too much trouble'.

Father Donnelly spluttered out his sip of tea and quickly constrained himself and said, 'Well, let me think now, and what date would that be?

Whereby, he was told it would be the 16 August, he then went directly to his diary and was given the time of 1.30pm which was his lunchtime normally, he was happy to oblige.

Bernadette was overwhelmed with Father Donnelly's caring character and his joyful sense of life and priorities. She was totally engaged in his conversation of marriage and sacred vows that went alongside such commitment.

She was transformed and Colm couldn't help but notice how focused and engaged she was in the conversation; she just kept asking more questions…

It was like Father Donnelly had totally transformed her. His methods of getting people to see things in a different light were certainly working on Bernadette.

As they left the Presbytery, Father Donnelly was convinced that he would see Bernadette again soon, and he wasn't wrong. She went back the next night to ask more questions, and she decided to convert to Catholicism and have her baptism.

Lena was concerned and approached Father Donnelly, and he once again reassured her mam, and she was also taken back by his philosophy of life and marriage. If it made Bernadette and Colm happy, then she was happy.

Bernadette turned to Serena for further guidance as she was a converted Catholic when she married Dylan a few years back.

As she sat with Serena and the twins, playing energetically on the floor with their toys. Serena began saying,

'It was rather daunting at first but he Journey of faith you go through before your wedding vows will set you up for life, it makes you complete'.

Bernadette was further resolved with the matter and couldn't wait for her wedding as she had now booked in with the church! And the Town Hall would be cancelled!

She then made her way to Colm's and told him everything, he was beside himself as he was holding his feelings back. The prospect of getting married in the Town Hall did not appeal to him really, but he was prepared to do it for Bernadette because he loved her so much and whatever she wanted he would give her.

However, he was so pleased to be married by Father Donnelly who had married his uncle, his Mam and Dad, his sister, and then after me there will be Niamh. It was meant to be.

One problem was left to be resolved, who would give Bernadette away, she wasn't that keen on Uncle Jake as he was such a grumpy soul.

'I have an idea my love, what about our Uncle John, he is a lively sort, and he does like us both, as he cuddled up to Bernadette.

She replied with joy in her eyes,

'Oh yes please pet, I hope he will agree to it.

Colm kissed her on the forehead and whispered in her ear, 'Of course he will', as he left her side and gave him call.

Uncle John was more than happy to oblige, and Sara his wife was more than happy as she was Matron of Honour of Niamh.

'Why don't I be Matron of Honour for Bernadette too' as she spoke out to Bernadette.

Bernadette was so happy about that as she only had her best friend Annette as bridesmaid.

Jacqueline entered the house and was overcome with emotion when she was told the new arrangements for the wedding. Her prayers had been answered; she couldn't be happier.

Niamh was upstairs and made her way to the living room as she could hear her mam with an elevated voice. She wanted to know what was going on.

Jack arrived soon after and as they sat around the dining table Niamh and Jack began whispering between themselves.

'What are you two whispering about, I need to know what is in conversation, please tell, right now? Said Colm urging them to reply.

They both said together,

'What would you think, if we got married alongside you two, a double wedding, would that be evasive, or would you just like us to prop you both up'. Niamh said jokingly.

Colm looked at Bernadette as she prompted Colm to answer,

'Well kids, you can come along for the ride, and we will look after you, promise'. Jacqueline began to cry, and Colm cuddled her. She got up from the Chair and said,

'There is still a box of sparkling wine at the bottom of the larder left over from Christmas, Colm go get a few bottles and we will celebrate this glorious day'.

As she composed herself the telephone rang out, it was Jason.

Jacqueline conveyed the marvellous news, and he was so happy for everyone, he would pop around directly. Just as he was finishing his conversation his doorbell rang, he told Jacqueline to hold on for a moment as he put the receiver down and made his way to front door.

As he opened the door, he was shocked to see Hazel standing there.

'What are you doing here? This is inappropriate behaviour coming to my home.

I think you need to go home right now', as he spoke loudly back to her. She responded in a pleading manner,

'I need to see you Jason, I need to tell you of my feelings'.

Jason was stunned by such a statement and responded directly...

'I will ask for you to be transferred tomorrow, and that is the end of our conversation. Good night', as he shut the door on her face

She stood a while and made her way back to her car and began plotting her revenge as she said to herself.

'He cannot treat me in this way; I won't allow it!'

He made his way to back to the telephone and told Jacqueline he would be with her promptly.

It was going to be a trying time for Jason, with this Hazel situation... he was alarmed by such behaviour. He hoped it would be a short-term crush and getting her transferred would be answer, but would it be.... ....

Chapter 10

As Jason awoke the next morning his first port of call was to the matron who oversaw the theatres. It was her prime responsibility, the duty of care towards the theatre assistants.

He marched straight to her office, it was 7.30am and she would be in the office dealing with staff Rota's at this time.

He knocked on the door and Mrs Shaw shouted directly, as she sat upright in her chair with her very starched nurse's cap which sat proficiently on top of her head.

'Come'.

'Good morning, Jason, as to what do I owe this pleasure at such an early start, she smiled back at him.

'May I', as he proceeded to sit down.

'Please' as she waved her hand in a courteous manner.

'I have come with some deep concerns about one of your theatre assistants' Hazel Cummings. She has conducted herself in an inappropriate manner by attending my home without my consent.

Furthermore, she has relayed some alarming comments towards me in a way that is not appropriate. I wish for her to be transferred as this is a serious matter of concern'

Matron, Mary Atkins, listened with the utmost shock displayed upon her face and concluded that she was in total agreement with Jason. She would speak to her directly and have her moved to orthopaedics as they are always advertising for staff either permanent or on secondment to fill their busy schedules.

Jason sat back for moment and conveyed his gratitude to Matron for acting so promptly in this matter. It was to take place with immediate effect.

He stood up and shook her hand; he couldn't help but comment on her firm handshake. She was woman of great talents, as her work rate was exceptional, having been at the hospital for twenty years. A much highly respected member of the team. Jason held her in high regard.

He walked out of the office with Matron towards Theatre 2 where he was operating that morning. Hazel would be replaced by Catherine who was just as capable as Hazel.

As they both approached Hazel as she walked slowly towards them. Matron spoke first,

'Please make your way to my office, I will be with you directly' Matron nodded to Jason with a stern expression on her face.

Hazel looked back to see if Jason was watching, she could only watch the back of his head as he entered through the theatre doors.

She slowly strolled alongside Matron and eventually entered her office. Matron conveyed the news to Hazel and informed her that this behaviour of hers would be documented on her file, and she was on a verbal warning. It was procedure, and if there were any further recurrence of such incidents, then she would receive a written warning.

She sat and mitigated her version of events stating that Jason had given out signs of encouragement. Matron was having none of it because she knew Jason's character and went on to say to Hazel.

'This is a good career move for you; it will give you experience of other specialities. All you need to do is work hard at it and keep yourself in good order young lady. Now, I suggest you make your way to your new department. I will let Matron Chatfield know you are on your way'.

Hazel stood up with a firm look on her face and left the office with caution and as soon as she got out of the corridor, she made her way to the ladies' room and checked no one was in there as she screamed loudly

'You piece of nothing, you nobody, I will have my day, I will have my say!'.

She smartened herself and proceeded to the Orthopaedic ward as if nothing had happened.

Her motion was that of calm and collectiveness, no one could decipher the underlying devious mannerisms she possessed. She kept everything hidden, her unnatural possessiveness for total control.

Could it be the abandonment her mother portrayed towards her as she left her at home by herself so she could go off to her tea parties and charity events. There were no feelings of love towards Hazel at all. Her mother didn't want children; she was told she was an unhappy accident that should never have occurred...

Her father was away most of the time as a salesman, he too, was work orientated and she never received any affection of love from him either. Just the odd smile and pat on the head like she was pet dog.

She became introverted and determined to make something of herself. The few boyfriends she had were scared off with her total possessiveness. One man in particular Mason, her last boyfriend, who told her to seek medical help after she had struck him with a pair of scissors that nearly marked him, but he grabbed them before impact. He implored her to see a doctor....

It had been a year since that incident, and she was binding her time nicely in her own mind, as she was totally convinced that Jason had strong feelings for her; he always greeted her with a warm smile and encouragement. The encouragement was that of work-related matters not of matters of the heart, but she couldn't distinguish between the two...

As her shift started in the Orthopaedic ward, she conducted herself in a warm-hearted way with such elegance as other members seem to warm to her straight away.

She could portray this caring warm personality for a while and then a devious character of rage would immerse, and she would then become this deranged person of complete hate and jealously towards others……. It took over her whole being. She had been able to contain it, but will she be able to keep this containment under control this time… Will it consume her completely… Only time will tell….

After her shift that day, she got into her car and made her way to Jacqueline's. It was easy for her to have pocketed Niamh's address when she was admitted. It was against the rules, but she didn't believe in any rules but her own.

She sat a little way down the coastal road and could just see the cottage.

'Oh! How quaint this little cottage is with its quaint little people in it', she muttered to herself.

Jacqueline at that moment came walking towards the cottage, she had just gotten off the bus. How she missed her lifts with Niamh to and from work, it would only be for another week or so as Niamh was itching to go back to work. However, it was refreshing to have that ten-minute walk home, as she smiled at herself. The view itself made up for it.

Hazel sat tentatively and made her mind up then that she would be seeing her and Jason again together in the not-too-distant future. She hadn't quite made her mind up yet on how to put an end to Jason and Jacqueline's relationship, but she will sleep on it for a while. Keep her cool head down and do as she is told at work for now…

As she sat a little longer, a car pulled up, and it was Jason's, her eyes widened with anticipation. She watched the front door of the cottage open as they lovingly embraced on the doorstep. Her jealous heart was in a rage; would her cool head explode. She was in turmoil, as she thumbed the steering wheel and bruised her finger with the force of the blow.

She pulled herself together as her heartbeat faster. Another car had arrived, and it was Colm.

'I cannot do anything here tonight. I must somehow get them alone' as she comprised her next steps to implement a perfect plan. She would write a note to both.

'Where is an isolated spot? She sat thoughtfully.

'I know, I will drive along the beachy head and find some romantic spot',

As she drove along the long road, she came across Marsden Cliffs with its bendy pathways so secrete. It was the ideal spot to demolish them…

'Oh! My so romantic for them', as she wickedly smiled back at herself through the wing mirror on her car.

'Let's just leave the love birds for a few weeks to enjoy each other and then I will pick the perfect night'.

She felt a gush of satisfaction within herself; she was practically ecstatic. Her mood was that of pure joy…

In the meantime, Jacqueline and Jason were discussing their plans for their marriage, which would be on Jacqueline's birthday the 4th of November.

A pre-Guy Fawkes wedding it will be. The house was full of marriage talk. Niamh and Colm couldn't be happier for their mother.

Jack, Niamh, Colm and Bernadette had their heads together as they discussed a joint wedding plan.

There would be a joint reception at the Stable Wood Hall for the four of them. They would have a word with Mr Andersby the manager, that evening. Colm would telephone him.

It turned out that Mr Andersby would be able to accommodate them as he suggested opening the next room as it was separated by sliding mahogany doors that can be open for extension.

Jason took Jacqueline outside for a moment and explained to her the situation with Hazel. As she stared into Jason's eyes,

'I am so shocked, she seemed a little off with me, but I put it down to how busy the hospital was that night when we attended with Niamh, but this Jason, how could she be so possessive with you?'

I can assure you love; I gave her no encouragement whatsoever on a personal note, I have, however, always encouraged her with work related matters. Do you think she totally misread my encouragement?'

'It seems so my love, but she is now transferred, so that should be the end of the matter.

As they sat huddled up in the garden, Jason kissed Jacqueline on the lips and whispered,

'I love you, soon to be my wife'.

They sat motionless watching the stars come out and nothing in their mind was going to interrupt their sense of completeness with one another.

Jason was in Theatre the next day so he would have a iced sparkling water, and Jacqueline went for a lovely glass of sparkling wine…

The night was full of calm and tranquillity, its essence transported across the sea as they watched the sliding of the frothy waves fold over like a package of everlasting love….

Chapter 11

The wedding plans were all set for the double wedding as they all sat outside,' The Straw Hat', a beach bistro situated on Beachy Head off the coast road towards South Shields. Colm wanted to make a speech as he stood up.

'I think it time to talk about, 'Stag Nights and 'Hen Nights folks, let's do it a week before the big day! to give us time to recover, let's face it Frankie's was nearly disaster', as they all laughed out loud,

'I second to that', as Jack stood up and lifted his pint to cheer the prospect of a week's grace before heading down the aisle.

Bernadette didn't want a big fuss about her hen do, and the girls were aware of that so the hen party would be to her liking, and she chose to go for a meal... As they all sat looking a little confused.

Annette, Bernadette's best friend from the art museum, spoke out,

'I think you are wrong! My dear friend: we must have a party before you get married even if it is a small party. What about, 'Jingles', it's a small jazz club, and I know you like jazz Bernie'.

Bernadette looked up with a pleased expression on her face, 'Oh yes, that sounds wonderful'.

They all raised their glasses and said, 'I will drink to that'.

Colm looked over to Bernadette and gave her an encouraging wink. The night was falling, and they made their way to the taxi stand on the corner of Benson Street.

It was getting a little chilly as the cool air whisked around the beach head, they huddled around the taxi stand shelter.

'Howay man! Where are the taxi's man!', Jack shouted out loud as he squeezed Niamh's waist. She was shivering now; he took his jacket off and placed it around her shoulders.

Two came around the corner, as they cheered with delight.

'I don't know about you guys, but I am having a good lie in tomorrow, well, it is Sunday', as Jack laid his head on Niamh's shoulder.

Colm spoke out sarcastically,

'I think you have forgotten something mate this Sunday we are all going to church as we are all getting married in church, we promised Father Donnelly. It's part of our journey of faith. It must be done', he gave out a wry smirk towards Jack...

"Aww man! I forgot about that; do we have to go every Sunday until we are married...? Said Jack, hoping for a reprieve.

Niamh wasn't giving him one,

'Yes, my pet, and you are going to enjoy it! Father Donnelly has a great sense of humour, and his mass isn't as bad I you may think'....

Jack looked at her with one eyebrow raised 'Are You having me on or is that true'.

'Would I lie to you? As she tilted her head towards him with her flirting look...

He recognised that look and was convinced it was going to be a good Sunday. Colm pointed out that they had not drank that much so they shouldn't have any sore heads in the morning.

The church service was a success, and Father Donnelly didn't disappoint... with his bouts of indirect accusations towards those who displayed a little reluctance to regular attendances at mass.

His conveyance was rather compelling because he used joyful anecdotes of wisdom to disguise the commitment. He always had the congregation smiling at his attempts.

They seemed to work every time, and he was grateful for the smiling faces on everyone's face.

As they left the church, Jack moved towards Jacqueline and Niamh and spoke, 'Wow, this guy is really something isn't he?'.

Jacqueline put her hand on Jack's shoulder and said,

'He certainly is, as he gives you so many options to explore, he doesn't force you to believe his words of wisdom, he just allays his presence on you, which is rather becoming. You get a sense of strength as you get drawn into that strength. It's a good thing in my view'.

They all walked along the coast road towards the beach to take in the Sunday morning air of discovery as they pondered along the sand each with thoughts of their own.

The dog walkers were strolling along the top pavement as they were not allowed on the beach between spring and summer periods.

'Oh, look there is Sara and John, let's go and join them', as Niamh spoke, Aww… They were sitting outside the café, 'The Beach Bow'

'Fancy seeing you here', Sara replied.

Jacqueline sat next to her sister and the rest followed on… towards their table.

Sara asked where they had all been and was astounded at the reply. She would only go to mass on feast days and the odd Sunday when Jacqueline prodded her in the back to accompany on some occasions. John was not fond of attending any church, only if Sara demanded it… which was usually for weddings, christenings… funerals…

They relayed the pre wedding plans to them and they were delighted to attend. John went on to say that he was invited to the stag night and was looking forward to it.

The day seemed to go so quickly and before they knew it, it was Monday, and it was time for work.

In the meantime, Hazel had set her plan perfectly to trap Jason and Jacqueline to Marsden Cliffs. How was she to know it was their favourite spot to meet… what a coincidence….

She had Jason's handwriting down to perfection, as she copied his signature several times. Jacqueline had signed in at the hospital, and she mischievously took a copy of her style of writing whilst the receptionist was busy with another member of staff.

She was ready to write her notes of deceit.

'Meet me at the Marsden Cliffs tonight, I think we should have a romantic evening, just the two of us, see you at 7pm, love you Jason'.

'Meet me at Marsden Cliffs tonight my love, I think we deserve a romantic evening, just the two of us, see you at 7pm, love Jacqueline'.

The handwritten notes were perfect, and she placed one in Jason's office, at lunch time. She then made her way to Jacqueline's cottage to push the handwritten note through the post box.

As Jason arrived back at his office, he was moved by such a loving note and didn't think to call to confirm, he was taken in by such a loving gesture.

When Jacqueline arrived home at 4.30pm she too was taken by the romantic note. 'Our favourite place', as she smiled with a delightful look upon her face.

It got too busy thereafter as she prepared tea for Colm and Niamh. It didn't occur to her to call Jason to confirm. The cliffs weren't that far to walk just 10 minutes from Jacqueline's cottage, and she couldn't wait to get along.

Hazel arrived home, she changed into her black running outfit and her black cap. She placed inside her holdall a kitchen knife. Her thoughts were conflicting as she kept changing her mind, but in the end, she made her way to the Marsden towards the cliffs...

She parked in the side street out of sight, but she had a good image of the walkway to the cliffs, and she would be able to see them when they arrived.

Jacqueline strolled down to the cliffs and took to the bendy road, and as she looked across to the car park, she caught sight of Jason's car. She was so excited to see him and smiled warmly towards him as he parked the car in the car park adjacent to Marsden Cliffs.

'Hello, my love', she said

He responded with,

'I loved your romantic note, what a great idea you came up with?'

Jacqueline looked confused for a moment and spoke

'What do you mean, you sent me the romantic note to meet you here, I too thought what a lovely idea'

Jason at this point looking a little alarmed

'I didn't write a note, and it seems you didn't either'.

As they stood with one another they heard a voice come past them, Hazel!

'Hello, you love birds, having a nice time are we, not for much longer!

She lunged towards Jacqueline to stab her, and she caught her arm slightly as Jason intervened and she stabbed him in his side as he lunged towards her. They tussled as Jason tried to retrieve the knife, but she went backwards and slipped onto a slimy rock and lost her balance. The waves swept her along as she went under the water….

Jacqueline managed to lift herself up as she moved towards Jason who was lying still. 'Oh! my love', she took off her cardigan and placed it firmly on the wound to try and stop it bleeding!

She quickly looked up to the pathway and caught a dog walker coming along and she screamed out!

'Help! Help! Please Help!

The dog walker made his way to them directly, and it wasn't long afterwards the Police and ambulance crew were called, and they arrived promptly at the scene.

Jacqueline conveyed to the Policeman the whole story. They moved quickly to get the divers into the water to locate Hazel, she wasn't visual. It looked as though she had drifted along the coast.

Jason was taken to surgery, and Jacqueline had a slight cut on her arm which was superficial. All she was concerned about was Jason.

The hours passed by and eventually Jacqueline received the good news, Jason was not too seriously injured, the cut was not as deep as anticipated. Jason had managed to stop Hazel from making a severe cut as she slipped on the slimy rock. It seems the rock had saved Jason, as he would make a full recovery.

Jacqueline cried out with relief and asked if the receptionist would mind calling her family, they will want to know. She called them directly, Colm, Niamh, and Emily, arrived shortly thereafter.

No one could take this all in, it was too bizarre to imagine... As Niamh went on to say,

'My goodness mam! She must be one disturbed lady mam, I dare not think of what could have happened'.

Jacqueline was only too pleased to hear Jason was safe; she couldn't bear losing another, she just couldn't comprehend that.

The divers were out all night and there was no sign of Hazel. They believed she must have been swept away by the waves. A further search would take place first thing in the morning. The divers would go further along the coastline....

Jason was sitting up in his hospital bed trying to make sense of it all. DCI Steele sat alongside him to gain a full recollection of the incident and to get a full background history of the attacker.

He relayed the up-to-date information with regards to Hazel.

'We have not ruled out that she may have survived, do you know if she was a good swimmer?'

Jason didn't and informed the inspector that it would be better to speak to some of his colleagues at the hospital, particularly the Theatre Assistants, one of them may know.

He left with his DS Clarke, and they pursued this next course of action, and it came to their attention that she was an athlete, she jogged, and she did swim and surf. The inspector believed at that point that there could be strong possibility that she may have been able to get herself safe along the coastline.

As he informed his team to put out an alert for this lady. The radio and newspapers were notified, and posters were made to be distributed throughout the city of South Shields and across the river to North Shields and Newcastle.

'Missing Hazel Cummings, please do not approach this lady, but call this number 0191 365 975 if you have any information about her whereabouts'

Chapter 12

As the daylight spun across the cloudy sky, it was a morning of fearful address in the Gibson household.

Niamh was quickly to the telephone to inform the Adult Centre that Jacqueline would not be teaching this week, and she would keep them posted of any further developments.

The Headteacher replied in a sympathetic tone.

'I am so sorry to hear such bad news, I do hope she is doing ok. Please inform her that she can take all the time she needs. We are all thinking of her and we will send a card with flowers to let her know she is thought of at this trying time'.

Niamh was delighted with the reply and would alert her school of the awful incident and would be in later this morning. She wanted to support her mam at the hospital as she was by Jason's bedside.

He was doing well and would be in hospital for at least another week to recover. Jason was not convinced and would rather recuperate at home, but he was told in no uncertain terms that he remains in hospital for another week.

Jacqueline was pleased with the stern response from Consultant Mr Jacobs. She felt he needed expert care, and he was going to get it.

It was all over the news this Tuesday morning and Hazel's best friend Natalie was overcome with shock and bewilderment. She had no idea that Hazel could be capable of such a thing. In her mind Hazel was a great friend, caring and thoughtful towards her.

As she sat listening to the news on the radio, she wondered if this had been provoked. Hazel had created this story of her and Jason being very close, and Natalie believed everything she was told. She had no reason to doubt her.

It was the cunning plan that Hazel had set down for herself. She believed that after she had stabbed them both she would be able to swim along to the end of the beach towards the beach huts which were correlated in numerical order. She knew that there would be one empty as Natalie had secured Number 4 this last year.

It was a relief to her that the beach huts were in her sights now as the sighted the correlation beginning with number 1 … not far now… and she made it to number 4.

She hadn't envisaged falling into the sea, but she was stunned by the rocky edge that cut along her thigh. It was momentary lapse, but she was able to make her way to the beach hut and lay low there.

As she awoke at 4am, it was time for her to retrieve her haversack which was well equipped with supplies and a change of clothes. It was a waiting game for her, as she lay silently near the rocky caves to make sure there was no one around. She sparred her chance and limped a little and made her way to her car.

'My keys! I haven't got my keys! They must have fell out of my pocket when I entered the water!'. She gasped with dismay ...

She went to boot of her car and picked up a stone nearby and banged on it so hard it dented the lock, but she managed to pry it open enough to get her bag as she pulled and pulled until it came free.

As she did so, a passerby in the distance, shouted towards her, but she had moved away and hurriedly limped her way back down to the caves hidden by the rocks…

It was a fair stretch to walk towards the beach huts; a few miles at least... She managed to bandage her leg and walked with a determined look on her face; it took her almost an hour. It was 5am. She breathed a sigh of relief as daylight beckoned, and the divers would be out once again…

Her thoughts turned to Natalie, her only hope of respite and recovery. She could work out what to do next when she arrived at Natalie's.

She changed her hairstyle and plaited it above her head. A complete change of clothing as she put her dress and sandals on. Her appearance was completely different, and it was risk to go out in the open, but she was confident no one would recognise her.

As she entered the local café which was opening. She ordered a croissant and coffee and smiled politely at the lady serving her who didn't bat an eyelid.

There was a sitting area outside and she sat calmly and took her time with her croissant. The train station was nearby, and she could be there within fifteen minutes. She gathered her thoughts and quickly composed herself and made her way to the train station.

As she walked confidently along the platform her train had pulled in, and she smiled at the guard as she boarded the train. He waved to the driver with his batten to signal all aboard and the train pulled away.

At this time the police had arrived at the train station as her train had pulled out, they had just missed their culprit as they posted her picture throughout the station.

She caught a glimpse of them and smiled wickedly through the glass window; her horrid persona was lurking in the background once more.

It wasn't long before she arrived at Natalie's. The door opened and Hazel greeted her with a hug as she put on the most innocent face.

'Come in Hazel, what on earth has happened, I cannot believe what I heard on the radio this morning, come, sit down and tell me all about it'

Hazel composed herself and came up with the most extraordinary tale, and it seemed to convince Natalie that she was telling the truth.

Her story was that Jacqueline was the jealous one and the vindictive one, she tells Natalie that it was Jacqueline that stabbed her in the leg, and it was Jacqueline alone who became enraged about Hazel and Jason supposed relationship.

Natalie pleaded with Hazel to go to the Police and tell her story. She asked Hazel if anyone at work could vouch for her to support her story.

Hazel went on to say.

'I could do that, not today, I just need to get some sleep, I am so tired', as she lay her head down on the sofa.

Natalie escorted her to the bedroom, and she left her there to sleep. She had to get to work at the local Coop, and she would be back at 4pm.

Hazel nodded to her and spoke

'See you later, thank you my dear friend'.

As Natalie left Hazel sat up in bed, she would not be able to stay here, it was only a matter of time before Natalie became suspicious. Her thoughts were muddled; she would get a few hours' sleep and head to the Building Society to draw out her savings.

A trip abroad to Canada maybe, I must think. Oh yes! My passport is in the glove compartment in the car, of course it is, I used it in the spring to visit Aunt Mary in Canada. Oh! thank goodness for that!

Two hours later, she entered the bathroom to freshen up and took out some of Natalie's make up. As she looked into the mirror and shouted out

'Oh! my life! Don't I look glamorous!'

Her thoughts of getting away seem to be rather comfortable now as she dressed herself in one of Natalie's outfit's, Jeans and a striped tee shirt and navy jacket. She picked up a rather fetching hat, that would almost cover her face.

'I am sure she won't mind, after all I am her best friend', as she sneered in the mirror.

I might as well take a few out-fits; I will leave her some money to compensate. Hazel began writing a letter, it was written with such conviction. It read,

Dear Natalie,
I am so distraught and unhappy, I must go to my aunt in Canada as she is so close to me and I can recuperate there. I do hope you understand. I have borrowed some of your things. I have left some money to compensate.
Thank you, my dear Friend. I will be in touch soon.
Hazel x

The Building Society was just about to open as she parked her car. When entering the building the assistant was very cooperative and gave her a slip to sign which read.

Withdrawal of the sum of £500.

Her happy mood had just begun as she entered Newcastle Airport there was a flight to Italy in two hours.

As she took a seat in the terminal, she sat looking dazed as she listened to a radio that was sounding out near her.

'A local surgeon has been stabbed near the lighthouse at the local beach near South Shields. He is recovering well with his fiancé who also was subjected to a superficial wound'. Posters of Hazel Cummings will be distributed throughout the Towns nearby …and nearby Airports.

Anyone who has any information about this lady please contact the police on 0191 365 975. Please do not approach this lady, she may be armed.

Her mind spiralled, as she made her way to the checkout desk. She kept her head down as best she could, and the gentleman opened her passport and noted the name Hazel Cummings; he did not want to alert suspicion and let her go through. She breathed heavily as she walked towards the passenger boarding bridge.

The attendant alerted the staff on the boarding bridge via their intercom service and as soon as she entered the boarding bridge, they asked her to step aside and come with them to a secluded office space.

She shouted back at them,

'What are you doing, what am I supposed to have done! I have done nothing wrong, I want to see a lawyer, I know my rights!'

The attendant responded in a calm manner,

'Yes, madame, if you just take a seat, someone will be with you shortly'

The door opened and there appeared DCI Steele who read out her rights and told her that she would be escorted to the police station; and there, she could then call her lawyer, or if she would like one appointed for her, namely, the Duty Solicitor on hand.

She abruptly replied,

'I will appoint my own Solicitor thank you!'

The DCI allowed her one phone call at the station, and she called Mr Kelsall a Solicitor who dealt with her conveyancing when she bought her flat two years ago. He advised her that he had no experience of criminal law, and the firm did not practice criminal law. He did, however, give her a reputable firm she could call. 'The Smith's firm on the high street.

She asked if that was possible and they pointed out she had her one call that was allowed.

'Please let me call this number or would you call it please'.

The DCI advised her that the Duty Solicitor was from the firm; Smythe's Solicitors'. She sighed and slumped her head down and replied.

'Alright'.

Mr Purvis was the Solicitor who would be representing her. A greyed hair tall gentleman who was well presented in his navy striped suit with a stiffed collared white shirt. His silk navy tie gave the impression that he was a notable Solicitor of worth. He entered the interview room to confer with his client, and he advised her to say, 'No comment'.

The interview convened and it was a pointless exercise, but Hazel was dying to spurt out that it was not her it was Jacqueline who caused the wounds to her and Jason. She had deluded herself that it was the truth.

She was taken to a cell to think things over, but it wouldn't be long before she became too agitated and let herself loose! from the 'No comment' syndrome.

Chapter 13

The following morning Hazel awoke as she slid on the hard mattress in her cell. The realisation of the serious nature of the charges that were put before her the day before started to take effect in her mind.

'How am I going to get out of this? I must convince them that it was Jacqueline who had first struck the blow with the knife. Afterall there were no witnesses, it's their word against mine', she smirked as she went to the basin directly in front her which was attached to the wall.

The cell door opened, and Mr Purvis informed her that she was to be interviewed for the second time. His instructions were the same, but she argued her case and told him her ambiguous tale that it was Jacqueline who was at fault.

Mr Purvis sat down and listened tentatively as she spun the yarn of deceit, and he himself was quite taken in by Hazel's innocent image of her girl who was set upon by two assailants? and the only way to defend herself was to fight back. She was becoming an infamous actor, who carefully portrayed the victim and not the villain…

As they both entered the interview room Hazel began to tell her astonishing story to DCI Steele. After the interview was conducted, DCI Steele instructed her to sign the statement of truth and did so without blinking.

She would be released on bail, pending further enquiries. Mr Purvis shook her hand and bid her good day. He left her with his card, and she was to get in touch with him again when further developments arose. An amicable handshake took place.

DCI Steele would bring Jacqueline and Jason in to get their version of events and get a statement to that effect from them both.

Jason was still in hospital and the DCI arrived by his bedside to ask him if he could shed some light on the recent events.

As he sat up in his bed, he began telling the DCI to question her colleagues, and other Doctors, as he was sure they would back him up on her precarious behaviour of late.

The DCI would follow this through and let him know the outcome in due course.

A further police car made its way to Jacqueline's. She answered the door and was most shocked at such a request and spoke out looking rather distraught.

'I am under arrest or something. I thought you had taken Hazel into custody. I have already told my version of events; I am due at the hospital to see Jason soon.'

The Policewoman carefully worded her response,

'You are not under arrest; we just want you to come down to the station to answer some further questions.'

Jacqueline arrived at the police station and was anxious to know why she was questioned once again.

DCI Steele arrived back at the station and informed her of the present developments. As she sat back in complete bewilderment listening to the tale of Hazel's side of the story. She couldn't take it in at first but went on to say with such confidence.

'You do know she is a manipulative pathological liar. She is completely obsessed with Jason. You do know that. You need to look deeper in her background because I think she must have done this before'.

DCI Steele gave her a warm smile and replied with sensitivity.

'I don't believe Hazel, but we must follow up with such accusations. We are asking the dog walker to come in. A Mr Manson, who telephoned the police about the incident. I am sure this will be cleared up shortly. Don't worry, we will get to the bottom of this'.

Jacqueline left the Police station and was informed that she would be driven to the hospital, it was the DCI who requested this. She was very grateful for that request.

She arrived back at the hospital in no time and sat tentatively on the chair annexed to Jason's bed. She put her hand on his and said,

'I am sure the dog walker must have seen who struck first. He must have seen something?'

Jason then turned towards Jacqueline and calmly spoke

'This is just a formality my love, the police must do their job, and I am sure it will be cleared up before long. Don't worry my love. I am going home tomorrow, and things will get back to normal, trust me'

Jacqueline looked back at him and couldn't believe how well he was taking this, and how well he was recovering. He was a man of strong character and wouldn't allow a manipulative person like Hazel to get the better of him.

The dog walker was located, and he was quite informative, in fact, he had witnessed the attack as he slowly walked his dog along the embankment that night.

When Jacqueline screamed help, he watched for a moment and then telephoned the Police. His version of events was that of Hazel had attempted to stab Jacqueline's arm and Jason intervened and they struggled, and she stabbed him in the side. The only thing he didn't witness was Hazel falling backwards. He had gone to telephone the Police by then.

DCI Steele requested DS Clarke, DC Chapman and WPC Henshall to pick up Hazel directly.

Hazel had made her way back to her apartment and was making plans once again to try and make a break for it. She knew in her mind it would only be a matter of time before they came after her once again.

She was too late! The doorbell rang and she tried to escape through the backyard, but DS Clarke was standing in wait, along with WPC Chapman.

'I want my lawyer Mr Purvis, here is his card, please call him now!' as she screamed at the WPC.

The WPC eventually got her into the police car as she resisted having the handcuffs on.

'Why are you doing this, I am not a criminal, I am the innocent party here', as she shouted in her face.

They arrived back at the Police Station and Mr Purvis her solicitor was called to attend yet again another interview with Hazel.

Mr Purvis interrupted his client throughout the interview and told her not to say anything that would incriminate her further. She reluctantly declined his request and began digging a hole for herself.

She was charged with Assault and was read her rights. He advised his client to plead guilty with diminished responsibility, she was not aware of what she was doing.

A Psychiatrist was to assess her, and it would be those findings that would establish her mental health during the attack on Jason and Jacqueline.

She was remanded in custody until the trial which would take place in the forthcoming months ahead.

Jason and Jacqueline were informed of the day's events by WPC Chapman.

They were both at home… and were sat in the garden and were so relieved that it was all over and they could now concentrate on the happy event ahead.

It was only a week away for the double wedding. Jacqueline had missed the hen party at the Jazz Club, it was a success, but she had far too much on her mind to think of enjoying herself.

Jason too had missed out on the boys' stag night; they all had a great time and nothing earth-shattering had happened. Colm made sure of that; he was not going down the road of Frankie's stag night. He had reminded Frankie of the past events and they both made a pact that this stag night was going to be merry but not overloaded with too much whiskey and brandy...

They both looked up at the stars and cuddled into each other and Jason spoke candidly.

'We can now start to build our future. I never asked you this, but would you consider living in the farmhouse, or would you want to buy another property'

Jacqueline turned to Jason with a loving glance and spoke,

'I kind of love your farmhouse, so I suppose it would be prudent to say yes'.

Jason was over the moon, as they sat discussing what to do with the cottage. Jacqueline knew of Niamh's search for an apartment in Marsden and she and Jack had found the perfect one near Marsden Bay.

Her thoughts turned to Colm, who was going to move in with Bernadette's mam for a short while until they found their feet.

'I will offer the cottage to Colm, obviously I will put it to Niamh and Emily first as it was their home too. I am sure they would love Colm to have it. that's if he wants it'.

Colm arrived home and Niamh followed on as Jacqueline gave them the news.

Niamh turned to Colm and spoke first

'I think you should bro, I think you and Bernadette would be so happy here and when we have party nights here, Jack and I can stay over'.

Colm looked at his sister and gave her a hug and kiss. Niamh responded,

'Wow my brother giving me a hug and a kiss together, that is going in my memory book'. As she gave her brother a wry smile with one eyebrow raised.

Jacqueline telephoned Emily and she was more than happy about the news, she answered with

'We are coming over in half an hour, let's celebrate'

Jacqueline was happy to receive such an offer, they all needed a celebration.

Bernadette had arrived and Colm took her into the kitchen to talk about the cottage. He explained that come November they could live here in the cottage.

'It would mean living with your mam until then, but we did say that we would find somewhere in a few months, didn't we? Are you happy with this, I want you to be happy'.

Bernadette couldn't believe it, the only problem she would have was when they left her mam's, it would be hard for her, being all alone in the house.

Colm suggested that she come to the cottage each week for tea to ease her way into being alone. Bernadette thought that would be a great idea. Let's just hope mam things so too.

The evening was full of joy and laughter. Jason was looking a little fatigued during the evening and it was said that he would stay the night. He didn't argue with that, he knew that he wasn't a 100%.

Colm and Bernadette decided to go over to her house and see her mam to have the talk. It wasn't that late, and she would still be up. Bernadette wanted Colm with her for moral support

Lena was most surprised to see Colm at 9.30pm. As she opened the door and let them in, she began to say,

'Oh, what has happened, it is always nice to see you Colm, it's getting late, it must be important I reckon', as she smiled at them both.

They all sat in the living room and Bernadette began telling her mam of what had occurred at Jacquelines.

She sat listening with a smile which turned slightly sad as they told her about their plans to live in the cottage and how excited they were. Bernadette loved the spot, the view, it was like a portrait to her, and she felt she would sketch away every week living there.

Lena responded to her daughter's enthusiasm as she looked into her gleaming eyes, she couldn't say out loud, 'I wish you would stay here', instead she replied in a warm manner.

'I am so happy for you both, I really am', as she kissed them both.

Colm pointed out energetically,

'We will be living with you for a few months, and I thank you for that Lena.

Well, I must be on my way home, busy day at the office tomorrow'.

Bernadette saw him to the door as Lena sat in the Livingroom. She spoke quietly to Colm,

'I am glad that is sorted, I love you, and we will be so happy'.

Colm kissed her goodnight and whispered, 'Love you more'.

Bernadette shut the door and made her way to her mam. She knew it was going to be hard, and Lena said goodnight to her daughter and went to bed.

She sat on her bed trying to come to terms with her daughter moving out, it had just hit her.

'I must not be selfish, I will cope, of course I will', she said to herself.

Chapter 14

Hazel was causing quite a disturbance at the Benson Police Station, based in Newcastle, screaming!

'You cannot lock me up like this, I am innocent, I am the victim here!'

Meanwhile, DCI Steele gathered speed on the investigation as his team had interviewed all the staff that were connected to Jason and Hazel and they all corroborated how Hazel had a fixation towards Jason....

Moreover, they also corroborated the same story of Hazel being too overly zealous with her attention towards Jason as she would block anyone trying to connect with him.

DCI Steele had all the evidence collated and whilst interviewing Natalie, her best friend, he noted that this young lady was a victim of total manipulation.

Natalie was shocked and confused about what she was told about Hazel and wondered if she had been too easily led by Hazel. She mentioned an incident when they first met some 12 months ago…

Hazel seemed pushy and insisted on giving her a lift. Natalie couldn't refuse as one of her tyres had blown out. How was she to know it was Hazel that had done the damage…. She thought it strange as the service on her car had only taken place that last week. The only thing she could come up with was that she had hit a bumpy spot of the brow of a hill the on that day…

DCI Steele was of the view that it was Hazel, but he couldn't prove that. The Psychiatric assessment was to take place this very afternoon and he was eager to know such outcome.

Mr Larkin the appointed Psychiatrist would be along presently, and she demanded a cup of tea and a sandwich.

Mr Larkin arrived, he was short gentleman, with a bald head. He was dressed in a brown suit with a rather fetching dicky bow which looked a little on the big side...

Hazel was the first to comment on such a garment, Mr Larkin was not deterred and sat back with a blank expression on his face and began asking her about her childhood.

She was bright and breezy with her response,

'I was lovely child, so loved and doted on, I wanted for nothing, I was precious'.

He sat watching her mannerism and writing down in detail his analysis. She further went on to say,

'I have no idea why I am here, they have made a fool of themselves, it will all come out. I will tell my story to the newspapers'

Mr Larkin diverted the conversation from her college days and ask her about relationships.

'I had lots of admirers, I played with them and when I got bored, I let them go. I was more interested in passing my exams and getting into the nursing profession. I am a caring person'.

As they both sat and went through the timeline of childhood and teenage life. Mr Larkin began the present time.

Hazel seemed to have a change of mood with the present time and came up with some conflicting scenarios. She told of her first job in the nursing profession where she was subjected to bullying and became introverted.

The truth was her first job in the nursing profession was in the children's trauma ward and she was greeted with such warm. She went on to the trauma department for adults because she wanted to learn more in the trauma department.

When asked about Jason, she cut herself off, as if everything had not occurred. She had dissociated herself from the present tense.

The assessment was concluded. Mr Larkin prepared his report and advised that she should be transferred to a specialised Psychiatric Unit for Dissociative Disorders.

DCI Steele was not surprised and agreed with his findings, but she needed to be under supervision 24/7 as she is still a dangerous threat to Jason and Jacqueline.

Hazel was reluctant to cooperate, and they had to sedate her to get the transfer completed.

DS Clarke called on Jason and Jacqueline to give them update on what had occurred this day and they both were so relieved that it was all over, and they could get on with their lives...

Jacqueline could now concentrate on her children's weddings. Niamh was having a little melt down over her dress as she wasn't sure she liked the veil; it was quite long.

'Let's get to the bridal shop, and try on the other veils, we have time, let's not panic' as Jacqueline spoke calmly to her daughter.

Niamh picked out a veil that was shoulder length, she felt so much better.

Bernadette was pleased with how Emily had made her dress; she would buy her a lovely painting from the gallery as a thank you.

Jacqueline wore a light mint suit to blend in with the bridesmaids, light pink dresses. Everyone was ready, the day was here.

Father Donnelly was dressed in his grand white Alb and Gold Chasuble. The service was commendable. The Father declined the reception invitation as usual. He always said,

'My job is done; you go forth and enjoy yourself'.

The speeches were illuminating as John jokingly told Bernadette that she was married to a forgetful man when it comes to possessions. As a child Colm would always go to school with a piece of toast in his mouth, but without his satchel. The toast was more important to him. He always forgets where he has put his keys…

'Don't let him forget you! pet, just prod him nicely'…

Dylan's speech was sentimental as he talked of Niamh his favourite niece, and Jack who he had come to know well now. He went on to say,

'A perfect catch, you reeled yourself in Jack and no mistake'.

Jack's mother Alice and his father Bob sat there with pride watching their son grow into a fine young man… They were more than happy to see him settled, their only son…

It was a special day indeed, as Jason and Jacqueline sat back and savoured the event and thoughts began to spill over of their forthcoming wedding.

Jason spoke of the barn for their reception.

'Are you sure my love, the barn is grand enough for you?' Jacqueline whispered,

'It's my kind of grand my love'.

They slipped away and went into the grounds and walked past the stables as they could hear the horses neighing in the background, simultaneously.

A seated area beyond was in sight as they sat and began to talk about the future. Jacqueline was of the view that they wouldn't need a housekeeper, but Jason pointed out that if she was going to be a constant babysitter she would have her hands full. Jason suggested that she come twice a week give the place a good once over.

Jacqueline admitted in the end it wasn't a bad idea, but I will be doing the cooking.

That is my area…

'Yes Boss', as Jason saluted her with a wry grin on his face They fell into each other with a loving kiss.

'We must get back and say our goodnights to everyone', Jacqueline said.

Lena sat in the corner, looking tearful as she was comforted by Annette.

'Don't worry Lena, they will be back with you in a few days, and you do have them until November'

Lena smiled back at her with no response. She was dreading going back to an empty house.

Jacqueline was astutely aware of Lena's expression and came to the rescue and spoke.

'Why don't you come to stay with me for a few days Lena? The house will be empty as Colm and Niamh will be off on their honeymoon; you can keep me company'.

Lena looked up surprised and said,

'Oh, I thought you would be at Jason's?'

Jacqueline pointed out that she didn't stay with Jason all the time and he was on call, so she always stayed home, it wasn't a problem.

Lena was delighted and Jason took her back to her house to gather her belongings. She was feeling rather upbeat about the whole situation now.

Jason said his goodnight to Jacqueline and couldn't help but notice what a woman I have in front of me. She thinks of everything and everyone.

The weekend went well in the cottage and Jacqueline began quizzing Lena about her hobbies. She in fact hadn't got any except for watching game shows on the TV.

She began investigating what she was good at before she was married. I used to like netball and swam a lot. My husband Duggie was the artist along with Bernadette. I used to knit a bit when I was younger.

Jacqueline managed to give Lena a weekend she would savour. They went swimming and got chatting with the swimming group. Lena was taken by the prospect of joining them on a long-term basis.

She also managed to fit in with a visit to Serena's, who talked incessantly about how she was coached by Emily to knit and cross stitch. Emily joined them later that Saturday evening and it was all settled. Lena was engrossed with such activities she didn't know where she was, but it was a nice place to be.

When Bernadette had arrived home with Colm, she couldn't stop talking. Bernadette was over the moon by such a change in her mam. She had worried so about her since the death of her dad.

Colm felt the relief too as he didn't want to leave in November on a sad note. He was so grateful to his mam and would tell her so.

Niamh and Jack finally decided to take their honeymoon in Italy, they were having the time of their life and took loads of pictures for everyone to see when they get back, they didn't want their honeymoon to end.

The weekend was over, and Colm and Bernadette had enjoyed their honeymoon weekend at the Grange Hotel. They would have a long holiday in Cornwall next year, as they weren't that keen of going abroad. It was known fact they were both money savers…

A week off work for Colm to enjoy his new surroundings as they began to plan the week ahead. Sketching on the beach. Lena could come along and have a swim, but she declined as she was going to meet up with the Swimming Group.

Colm and Bernadette had their style of a honeymoon at Sandhaven Beach, which they loved so much.

As they sat near the enclosed cove, which was a romantic spot, the sand was so silky and the waved caressed the side of the rocks.

They lay together so blissfully; a woven bliss of happiness…

Chapter 15

How Jacqueline was finding this calming sensation surrounding her, no drama, no fuss, just complete calm and serenity.

She stood in the garden looking out at the surfers on the beach; a kind of watchful peace as she stood a while.

A voice in the background distracted her for a moment, as she looked sideways. It was Serena shouting towards her, as she pushed the twin pushchair towards the garden gate.

'Hello Jacqueline, I thought I would call on you to see if you fancied a walk along the front with these two joyful creatures, as Serena stroked the heads of her twins, Amy and Ethan. They responded with their usual baby talk, as they squealed merrily away.

Jacqueline was delighted to take a turn along the seafront and responded energetically to the invite.

'It's definitely the morning for it, with all this lovely sunshine beaming away' They stopped off at the ice cream parlour Menchello's and took a seat outside.

Serena enquired how things were after the terrible ordeal with Hazel. As Jacqueline frowned a little, as she said,

'Yes, it's a pleasing outcome and Jason and I are so happy to see the back of her, I hope she gets the help she needs to be honest. I couldn't believe how devious she had become. I had no idea!

Serena answered looking subdued,

'I hope that unit is secure, as she sounds like the type to escape if the opportunity arose. I hope I have startled you with that remark. Anyway, I am sure she will get the medication and help, and it will turn out well for all concerned'

It hadn't occurred to Jacqueline of such a notion, but she was advised the Secure Unit in Durham was highly secure.

She didn't think any more of it as she changed the subject back to the twins.

They were coming up to nine months now and Amy was raring to go, as she was now walking around the furniture. Serena was animated by the conversation and relayed the happy occurrences of when Amy decided now is the time.

'Oh, Jacqueline you should have seen her, she was excited at first but when she plopped down on her bottom, she left it for a few days, but now she keeps going around the sofa and back.

Ethan sits quietly watching her, he is not so ambitious, I think he likes to ponder and take is time…. He is crawling a lot these days, so maybe he may follow in her footsteps later'.

Jacqueline replied with a joyful smile on her face.

'Oh, I cannot believe how grown they are, such bonny bairns. I love the dark curls of Amy, and it looks like Ethan has a few coming too. It won't be long before Emily is having her baby'

'Is Emily having a home birth, or does she prefer the hospital', asked Serena.

'Oh, she is definitely going to the hospital as Frankie wouldn't be able to cope, I don't think, from what I can gather' as Jacqueline smiled back at Serena.

Serena was itching to know about Jason and herself as she finished off her ice cream cone,

'So, how is Jason, how are the wedding plans going, I am dying to know more'

Jacqueline raised her right eyebrow as she spoke

'I bet you are, yes, we are doing fine. Everything will be fine for November, our wedding day, the 4th of November.'

Serena sat up rather spritely and leaned into Jacqueline,

'I see, you have already set a date, that is great news, I will pop that in my diary' as she winked at Jacqueline with a wry smirk on her face.

The twins began to twitch and move their arms around.
It's nearly time for their dinner, they know are to get your attention. Well, it's been a lovely stroll and thank you for the ice cream cone, but I must get back with these two lovelies' as Serena said her goodbyes to Jacqueline.

Jacqueline was in the mood for a long stroll along the beach as she watched the surfers and the families come out in droves with their deck chairs and picnic baskets.

The queue at Collette's Fish & Chip Hut was getting bigger by the minute as lots of people stood patiently waiting for the glorious Fish & Chips. They were always delicious, fresh fish, catch of the day and beautiful chips cooked in beef dripping.

She strolled past the queue and made her way on the silky sand, barefoot as she put her plimsoles in her yellow striped canvas bag.

Her mind drifted to yester year when her mam and dad were alive. It was the busyness of the beach that reflected her childhood.

She reminisced as she brushed her feet into the sand slowly. The vivid memory of her dad playing beach tennis with her with their little bat and ball and how she loved to win over him. 'Oh, how competitive I was', as she smiled to herself.

Her mam sitting busy getting the picnic ready on the tartan blanket. Those quaint tins full of sandwiches, egg and cress, cheese and tomato, and mam's favourite salmon and cucumber. Not forgetting mam's homemade bacon and egg pie and orange cordial to drink.

Jacqueline was transported to that wonderful day on the beach with her parents and sisters. That vivid memory had not struck her for years. 'It must be the image of all these families and children that have revived my memory', she thought to herself.

Looking rather dazed and not quite in the present, she sat down on the sand for a moment to gather herself.

She smiled at herself thinking now of her future as she stared into the sea and how romantic it looked to her,

> As the sea sets its dazzling caress
> It folds into a sublime mountain to possess....

As she sat watching the waves as they rose up like a God-like creature; she got lost in the poetic movement of the sea touching the sandy shoreline.

She felt a little tap on her shoulder and there stood Father Donnelly, 'Where are you? Lost in your imagination I see'

Jacqueline stood up and answered back

'Yes, Father, it's so romantic the sea, don't you think?'

'I don't know about romantic, but it is certainly fascinating how it resonates such curves at such a height...' as he tilted his trilby at her Jacqueline.

'Walk with me Jacqueline, let's have a little catch up'

He enquired about her well-being and the family. Jacqueline was quick to assure him that everything was going well.

'I am pleased to hear that', said he.

They walked to the promenade and sat for a moment, and Father Donnelly began asking about Hazel.

She was optimistic about the outcome and conveyed the situation to him in a light-hearted way, to avert how she still felt a little uneasy, but she was sure it would pass in time.

He politely tipped his trilby and bid Jacqueline a good afternoon, as he went about his church business.

Jacqueline gave him a warm smile and told him not to overdo things, he was now in his later life, but you wouldn't think so, for how many miles he covers each day walking and visiting his parishioners.

She cheerfully walked briskly back to the cottage to tidy up and make a celebratory dinner for the return of Niamh and Jack from their honeymoon.

They will be due back in five hours' time.

Emily waved to her mam as she passed her on the road. She pulled up and Jacqueline was elated to see her so early.

'My, you are growing so, and blooming well, pregnancy definitely suits you pet' as Jacqueline smiled at her daughter.

Emily answered with a little sigh,

'I know mam, but I won't be able to drive much longer, I am finding it rather hard getting in and out of the car now. So, I am going to stop next week, Frankie's orders'

'That's not a bad idea pet, only few months left', as she gave her daughter an assuring look.

They went into the cottage and Emily put her feet up for a while as Jacqueline made her a nice cup of tea.

Emily was so looking forward to seeing her sister and shouted to her mam 'I bet she has a great tan mam; I am so jealous'

Jacqueline came into the living room and spoke

'You, my pet, have nothing to be jealous of, you are going to be too busy soon to be jealous about anything'

Emily was excited and couldn't wait for these next few months to go over as she patted her stomach.

The buffet was all ready for them to arrive, and all the family were there. The house was buzzing with conversation, and the twins were happily transported into their play pen with lots of toys to keep them occupied.

Amy, however, looked as if she was trying to get out of the play pen, she was itching to try out the sofa. How she loved walking around a sofa...

'They're here! Shouted Colm

He quickly dashed to door to welcome them. Niamh was so brown and Jack too, they looked so continental in their summer outfits and summer hats.

'Look at you sis, wow, looks like you have had a great time'. As Colm winked at Jack. He reciprocated with a wry smile on his face.

Jacqueline got up to greet her daughter and was happy to see them home safe. How she worried about them flying! The relief on her face said it all…

Niamh sat next to her sister Emily and hugged her with such love.

'I have bought you and Frankie something special from Italy for the baby. An Italian spiral fur toys that can be attached to a pram'

Emily and Frankie were delighted with such a gift.

Everyone was dying to see the photos. Niamh regrettably told them they have all the films, but had not had them developed yet… and went on to say,

'We didn't have time to get them developed', as she smiled at Jack Dylan who then came into the conversation and spoke out

'I should think not!' wink wink….

The house was full of blissful love and togetherness….

Chapter 16

Hazel began getting acquainted with her new surroundings in Dunston HMP Psychiatric Unit... The Secured Unit was well staffed. It wasn't long before she made herself known to many of the inmates. There was one inmate who stood out in her mind, Pamela Statham a tall girl, very thin, with mousy straggled hair. She was quite taken with Hazel as they buddied up at mealtimes.

As they sat eating their fish and vegetables, Hazel began to draw Pamela in by asking if anyone had ever escaped from this unit.

Pamela looked up and said,

'Oh, yes, there is always someone trying to get out, but they never succeed, too many guards everywhere'.

Hazel sat for moment and began thinking of how she could manipulate one of the guards. Her warm and smiley persona seem to materialise as she scouted around to see if any one of them looked like a good victim...

It wasn't long before she decided to get over friendly with Robert Carson, a muscular man with rugged features.

He humoured Hazel, with her flirtatious outbursts, he was fully aware of how some prisoners would use their flirty mannerisms to get what they want. He had been with the Prison Service for twelve years and seen it all; he was no fool.

Pamela pointed out to Hazel that she was barking up the wrong tree with Robert and she should flout her attentions towards Adrian Simpson; he was a sucker for a woman with good looks and loved the flirty inmates. He thrived on the attention...

Hazel eyes widened with the prospect of getting out of the unit before long, she would bide her time and reel him in...

She couldn't sleep that night, tomorrow was visiting day, and she knew Natalie would be coming, as she was on the visiting list.

The dawn broke, not that she could see much of it because of the barred windows in her room. She expressed herself by speaking out loudly through the hatched door.

'A bit of fresh air wouldn't go amiss, I am suffocating in here, do you hear me!'

Adrian, one of the guards came to the hatched door and pulled it open with a stern look on face as he said.

'You know the rules Hazel', he suggested a turn around the garden. Hazel smirked back at him before she answered,

'You call that a garden it all fenced in! with barbed wire, that's not a proper garden and you know it'.

Adrian told her settle down and get ready for breakfast; if you behave yourself girl, you could get a transfer to an open room with windows, that's for the well-behaved patients.

Hazel jumped up and made her way to the hatch, and smiled warmly at Adrian and spoke in a soft tone

'I am good girl, I am a very good girl, how long before I get a move to one of these open rooms', as she flirted with Adrian touching his face and mouth and pouting her lips at him.

He stood there for a moment and continued to enjoy this intimate connection with Hazel. As he moved into the hatched door she kissed him on the lips. He responded well and by saying

'You have luscious lips pet, I wish to see more of them, later'

Another guard was coming down the corridor, and he swiftly closed the hatch. Hazel quickly made her way to the basin to watch her mouth out, as she looked in the mirror, she smiled at herself,

'What a revolting man! His breath smells like a cess pit! I will have to keep this up for some time, I must... as she sat back on her bed...'

It was now visiting time, and Natalie, her only loyal friend, was prompt as ever. She asked her how they were treating her and if she needed anything.

Hazel was gasping to find out how Jason was and what was happening at home. Natalie informed her that Jason made a full recovery, and their engagement was announced in the local gazette. The wedding was to take place in November.

She sat motionless as she listened to Natalie, her body froze. Her mind moved quickly from the subject as she asked Natalie to bring her some new make-up and could she bring her some clothes.

'Can you bring me my black dress and halter neck navy blue dress, and my sling backed shoes, they are in my wardrobe. Can you do that for me, as she gave Natalie her innocent pleading look.

She was more than happy to help Hazel, and she would bring them next week. The visit was over, and they said their goodbyes.

Hazel went to her therapy classes and interacted with everyone. She portrayed this caring thoughtful persona throughout the sessions and told herself to continue doing so until she was transferred. Everyone was interacting with her, and it didn't go unnoticed by the staff. They were to log every session of behaviour, and it looked promising so far.

She went to her room and counted the days off to when Natalie would return with her clothes.

She was determined to get moved and to escape. As she lay on the bed to plan and plot her next move...

The earlier conversation with Adrian sprung in her mind when he let her know that he would come to visit her in the early hours as he was on the night shift.

She had a pastel dress which should be worn with a slip underneath, but she wouldn't be wearing a slip underneath that tonight. Her mission was to get Adrian fully engaged with her, and she would stop at nothing, even if it was too distasteful.

'I must lure him in, that is the only way to get out of here'

As she lay in wait, and watched the clock, it struck, 3am and the door slowly opened, and in walked Adrian.

She lay there and beckoned him to her, and he was a willing victim. He got on top of her and started to undo his trousers, rubbing his hands all over her. He kissed with such force. She slowed him down and asked him to sit up for a while.

'Let's just take our time Adrian, there is no rush. We should get to know each other better'.

He got up off the bed and stood up looking rather frazzled and uncomfortable for a moment.

'I think I may have rushed things a little, you are so dammed attractive Hazel. I thought you wanted it as much as I did'

Hazel smiled back at him,

'I do Adrian, but I would like to get to know you. I don't want our relationship to be casual'

Adrian looked on with surprise.

'We can still be intimate and get to know each other as he eagerly awaited her response'.

She let him know that it was that time of the month and perhaps they should wait a few days and get to know each other.

He put his arms around Hazel and bent her head back and kissed her again forcibly and she responded.

'Let's just lay here for a while, shall we'

They lay for another hour as he fondled her body and she cringed inside, smiling away. It was time he went on his rounds. He didn't want to cause suspicion, not at this stage.

He said goodnight to Hazel as he pulled her into him, and she felt that she would have to respond to keep him on her side.

They stood for moment, and he left her with these words,

'We are going to have such a good time Hazel, such a good time'…

As the door shut, she held herself for a moment and then hurriedly took off all her clothes to wash herself all over.

'I must go to Jason he will come round, once I see him again, we will be together. I know he loves me '….

The next day she had her session with her appointed Doctor who was Dr Laxton. He went through her attendance sheet and noted the comments from all the therapy groups and asked Hazel how she was feeling.

'I am feeling rather good Doctor, they are all so nice here'

He asked her questions about the attack on Jason and Jacqueline and probed her further on the subject.

'Can you talk me through why you were brought here?'

She looked confused for a moment and then spoke,

'I was stupid, but I was provoked, I am not a bad person'

Dr Laxton noted the dissociation of her character, but it was early days before she would be able to bring herself to be accountable for her actions.

'We shall leave it there for today, Hazel'

She made her way to the wing with Robert, the guard who was assisting her back to her room.

'I would like a turn in the garden Robert for some fresh air, is that allowed? As she turned to him with her innocent look.

He smiled back and spoke

'Yes, it is allowed after a session, it's good to get some fresh air in your lungs.'

They talked about the weather and Robert's family, and he was open with the discussions about his wife and children.

Hazel listened and thought,

'That will be me and Jason with children soon'.

The day passed by, and nightfall came, and Hazel was not looking forward to Adrian's visit.

'I must fend him off somehow, but for how long will I be able to do this?'

Adrian's footsteps came along the corridor and just before he was about to open her door, one of the assistants further down the wing shouted to him

'I need your help with Simon; he is getting himself in a state'.

Hazel heard the voices and was so relieved when Adrian's footsteps were no longer....

Chapter 17

It was time for Hazel to put her next plan of action to the test. As the drugs trolley buckled along the corridor with its old-fashioned cast-iron wheels; she seized the moment when the nurse was distracted with another patient. There were lots of bottles of medicines on display and she grabbed the sleeping pills, and a bottle of antihistamines. As the nurse returned to the trolley she shouted to Hazel,

'Well, this is a first Hazel', you are usually reluctant to come and get your medicine, Glad to see you are settling down'

Hazel portrayed her infamous conniving smile, as she stood with a triumphant expression on her face, and began saying with a look of innocence ….

'Yes, I am starting to feel much better now, thank you, it's all down to you Nurse Chambers'.

Her plan was working out nicely; she would set the trap for Adrian tonight as she lures him in…

The nightfall came quickly, as she dressed herself in her black dress and Adrian was eager to get to her room, as he opened the door, he stood staring and said,

'Wow, you have made such an effort for our big night, let's get that dress off shall we'.

Hazel spoke,

'Wait, wait, I have made a big effort Adrian, now you must reciprocate. Let's go to your place, this bed is too small for the both of us, and it is our big night', as she pouted her lips at him….

Adrian stood for moment; his mind was reeling. He wasn't going to miss this opportunity of having his way with Hazel tonight as he spoke out,

'Okay my pet, just hang fire and I will check if the coast is clear and we can go through the back door. I will go and fetch the outdoor keys'

Hazel was elated with the response; she could now get her bag together and pack a few things. She squeezed as much as she could in her bag.

Adrian returned and they made their way to his flat which was a mile down the road, as they entered the flat Adrian pounced on her as she pulled him back and said,

'Hey, what about some drinks and some music, let's do this properly shall we' He smiled back her,

'A glass of wine my pet'

'Yes, please, that would be lovely'

When he returned with the drinks he went over to the radiogram and put a record on, and when his back was turned, Hazel quickly took the plastic bag out of her handbag. The tablets were already finely crushed, and she poured the contents into his drink. There were enough tablets in there to keep him out for the rest of the night.

They sat on the sofa and Hazel kept him chatting away as he drank his wine and just as he was about to make his move, he fell on Hazel, and she quickly removed herself off the sofa. She looked back at him with revolt,

'There, there, you nasty nobody, sleep tight'.

She scoured the flat and found some money, quite a lot of money!! £100. She placed it in her bag and noted the car keys in the dish by the front door.

'How nice of him to leave his keys in plain sight'.

Her journey back to South Shields had begun and she would make her way to Natalie's and tell her a different story.

As she pulled up outside Natalie's the light was on, and she was home. 'Oh, thank goodness for that', as she said herself.

Natalie opened the door to a tearful Hazel.

'Oh, my goodness, Hazel what has happened your dress is torn, let's get you in'

Hazel made a tear in the dress to look like she had been assaulted. She began telling her extraordinary story,

'Natalie, you have no idea, the guard dressed me up like this and assaulted me.

When he left my room, I managed to get out and make my way to yours.' 'Have you changed your car; I thought you had a red mini?'

'I changed it a little while ago, I got a good deal on the black mini'

She began crying again, with her sorrowful look and pleaded with Natalie not to do anything because it was her word against his and she would much rather forget it about it and stay with her for a while.

Natalie in her naivety believed every word she said, and was happy to help…

As Hazel slept in the spare room, she began thinking about Jason; how would she persuade him that she was the one for him. The fixation was getting out of hand, and she realised that Adrian would be awake the next day, and alarm bells would ring. She needed to act fast.

Jason and Jacqueline were comfortably snuggled up on the sofa at his farmhouse, near Seaham. It was a lovely place to live as Jacqueline looked around.

'I think my love, this is the perfect home, for me', as she kissed Jason on the mouth.

'Are you sure my love, because it's a bit out the way'

'I have spoken with Emily and she and Frankie are happy to drive here with the little one when it's my turn to take over. Emily says it's only twenty-five-minute drive, she loves driving'.

Jason moved his arm and placed it around Jacqueline's waist and drew her into him and they passionately embraced.

'I think it's time we went to bed, as he pulled Jacqueline up'

She was happy with his response, and they had a loving night together…

The next day, Jason was not due at the hospital until later that day and Jacqueline was enjoying the summer break from the Adult Centre. She would make them a hearty breakfast as they both were feeling rather peckish.

'Let's sit in the garden shall we and enjoy our breakfast outside, I love your view of the lake it so peaceful and tranquil', as she turned to Jason.

'Yes, it's my favourite spot here, it's where I do all my thinking.' 'What are you thinking right now'

'I am thinking how dammed lucky I am to have such a wonderful person in my life as you'

They sat talking about the farmhouse and its decoration and Jacqueline was only too happy to renovate it, as it was rather dowdy and needed a complete makeover. Jason was more than happy for Jacqueline to take the lead on this as she couldn't stop talking about what she had in mind.

'Bright colours are needed, with an image of freshness and light to show off all the glorious rooms you have my love'

Jason was in complete agreement. He just wasn't bothered with the farmhouse living on his own and now it would be a proper home as he beamed with joy.

Meanwhile, Hazel was beaming with joy as Natalie left for work, and she telephoned the hospital to enquire whether Jason was on shift. She disguised her voice and said she was Jason's sister, and they informed her that he wouldn't be in until later.

She answered,

'Ah, that's fine, I will call him at home'

She got into Adrian's car and was grateful the tank was full of petrol as she made her way to Jason's.

Adrian at this time awoke from his deep sleep and couldn't stand up properly for a moment. It wasn't long before he realised, he had been drugged. He went into the bathroom and washed himself as he tried to remember what happened.

'It must have been in the wine, when I put the record on, that's the only time she could have done it. Oh, what a mess, what am I going to tell them. I cannot tell them the truth. I will play it down'

He then realised his car had gone as he screamed'

'You bitch; I will make sure you get what's coming to you'

He had a few hours before his shift began and would call for a taxi. As he picked up his wallet he couldn't believe she had taken his money too, that was his wages for the month!

'I will have to use the gas bill money, good job I put that in the jar, I hope it's still there' as he sighed with relief at the £20 sitting in the jar.

He kept a low profile when he arrived at work and he was informed by some of his colleagues that she had escaped and his response was,

'I thought she was rather deviant, written all over her'

Hazel was fast approaching Jason's and could see his car parked. A little pause as she looked at herself in the car mirror and smiled...

As she got out of the car, she rang doorbell, but there was no answer. They couldn't hear it at the back. The garden was large, and they were seated at the far end.

She walked to the side of the farmhouse to the side gate and walked along the craggy path until she caught sight of him. Her heart was pounding! As she took a step back and pondered for a moment.

Her mind became so dissociated with the reality of the situation; she just walked straight into the garden. Her eyes were pinned on Jason, it was if Jacqueline wasn't there, she didn't exist.

'Hello my love'

Jason looked around in horror, he put Jacqueline behind to protect her and calmly answered in a warm tone so as not to divert her. Jacqueline at this point noted the little gate behind her and would make a dash for it. She whispered in Jason's ear

'Keep her talking I am going to get out the gate next to me'

Jason calmly went towards Hazel and warmly responded to her 'Are you alright, Hazel, can I get you anything pet'

Hazel warmed to the suggestion and at this time Jacqueline was out the back and went straight to the telephone box. She dialled 999!

Jason kept Hazel occupied and asked her to sit awhile and poured her some tea from the garden table. She was rather liking this attention, and it wasn't long after that the Police arrived to save the day.

She was handcuffed by DS Clarke and escorted to the ambulance waiting outside. Her head quickly turned towards Jason. Her face looked triumphant in a strange sort of way as she spoke out,

'See you soon my love'

Jason felt so sorry for her at that point, he wondered what had occurred in her life to make her this way. He truly hoped she would get the right help this time.

Jacqueline cried with relief, Jason was safe, and they could now finally get on with their future.

Chapter 18

It was apparent to all that Hazel needed to be secured in a unit out of the area completely.

After a further assessment of her ill health, it was agreed she would be transferred to a specialist wing in Surrey. The facilities at this practice were well suited to cater for Hazel's dissociative disorder.

Natalie would not give up on her best friend and would give her as much support as she needed. She decided to visit Jason and offer her heartfelt excuses on behalf of Hazel. Jason empathised with Natalie and conveyed his best wishes and hoped the situation would render itself for the better, for all parties concerned.

Jacqueline, however, was not at this point feeling that empathy and kept her own counsel for fear of upsetting Natalie.

She went back into the house and left Jason to show her to the door. As he returned to Jacqueline in the kitchen, he looked a little concerned about Jacqueline.

'Are you alright my pet, I know this has been an awful ordeal'

'It's just that I cannot get over her eyes the way she looked at you, it was like she was devouring you. It was rather scary, my love'

'I think her illness is far more severe than one anticipated and I think now she will get better treatment at this specialist unit.

My concern is you, my love, and I will do my best to divert you back to happier times'

As he went on further to say,

'We should take a trip to the DYI stores and start picking out paint and paper for the renovations. I am going to give Ronnie our maintenance man a call. He used to run things here at the farm when it was a going concern. He will get the renovations done quicker than we ever could. Your job, my love is to pick out all what you desire'

Jacqueline's mood lifted somewhat as she energetically spoke,

'I must go to our Emily's haberdashery to pick out the right materials for new curtains, and we could pick out some paintings from the art shop. I would love to include one of Serena's framed portraits of cross stitch landscapes. They are so original far superior to a painting in my view. If that's alright with you my love'

Jason laughed out loud,

'That's my girl, getting things done', as he hugged her tightly.

They went off to the DYI store in Newcastle and picked out some bright pastel colours for the walls and some delightful wallpaper for the living room. It was the beige background and a gold pear shaped design on a particular roll of wallpaper that caught their eye, it looked rather striking as they stood back and admired it.

The shop assistant allowed them to take a sample piece of wallpaper so they could get a better picture visually on their wall. Jacqueline felt it would give them a better perspective. She liked things coordinated, the matching up of wallpaper and curtains was so important to her as she felt it affected the whole look of the room.

After hours of shopping around, they made their way to the tea rooms for a relaxing cup of tea and some of their delicious tea buns.

She was elevated and felt the morning was a success after all and would call on Emily presently to see how she was doing.

As they arrived at the Haberdashery shop, Belinda the manager now had notified her that Emily was staying home today and putting her feet up.

Jacqueline looked a little alarmed as she felt Emily would have told her they spoke on the telephone each night. She thanked Belinda and didn't want to browse around the shop; she just wanted to get to Emily's to make sure everything was alright.

Jason calmly said to Jacqueline,

'It will be alright darling; she must be coming up to eight months. She should be at home resting up'

Jacqueline spoke out,

'Yes, I know, she has just passed eight months. I kept telling her to stay home, but she insisted she was feeling great and was only in the shop a few hours a day. I just want to make sure everything is alright'.

It wasn't long before they arrived at Emily's. They rang the doorbell but there was no answer. Jacqueline looked through the window, and no one was home. She was getting worried now.

Jason calmly escorted to the car and said they would make their way to the hospital, maybe she has a check-up today. Jacqueline knew that wasn't the case, she would know about that appointment.

They arrived at the hospital and made their way to the maternity department Jason went directly to Mr. Robson, the obstetrician, to see if he knew anything about Emily today.

Mr. Robson gladly notified them both that Emily was admitted an hour ago as she had high blood pressure and they would be keeping her in for a few days. The swelling of her legs and feet needed to come down too. She and the baby were resting and doing fine as he smiled at them both.

'Let me take you along to her now, I am sure she will be happy to see you' Frankie was by her bedside and looked up,

'Jacqueline, I was just about to call you once Emily was settled, but you are here now'

Emily smiled at her mam,

'It's alright mam, I am doing fine, I was a bit scared at first. I thought I was having contractions, but it was indigestion. I just need to get my blood pressure down; I think I panicked a bit'.

Jacqueline was relieved to hear it, and they sat and talked about the renovations to the farmhouse. Emily got excited and Jacqueline explained to her not to get too exertive.

'It won't be long until it's the real thing, pet, so you get some rest now and take notice of what Mr. Robson tells you, 'As Jacqueline kissed her goodbye.

Frankie saw them out, he looked a little pale, and Jacqueline told him not to worry. 'She will be fine Frankie, you get some rest too lad, you look like you could with it'

'I will get my head down on the big lounge chair next to her. I don't want to leave her just yet'.

It was in the early hours that Mr. Robson was alerted to attend Emily's room. Her temperature was taken, and it was 38c (100.4F) which suggested she had fever. It looked like she had contracted some kind of viral infection, and this needed to be treated immediately.

The concern was the high blood pressure and the slow contractions that seem to have developed in the meantime. It was going to be a busy night.

As they intravenously injected the antibiotics into her and checked the baby's heartbeat, it was beating regularly. It became apparent that stabilisation was the key in next twelve hours. Mr. Robson's concern was that of delivering the baby, which looked imminent within the next twenty-four hours.

The next morning, Emily's fever had come down slightly, so the antibiotics were working, and her blood pressure had stabilised now.

The nurse who was due to come on duty that morning had rang in sick and Colleen the night nurse came forward and said she would stay on to assist. She was a dedicated nurse and would not let the team down. Mr. Robson appreciated her commitment to the situation.

By this time Frankie and Jacqueline were alerted to the situation and Jason accompanied them to the hospital. If offered his services to Mr. Robson who gladly accepted as he could do with another pair of experienced hands.

It was now time to get Emily transferred down to the delivery suite and monitor the progress of mother and baby.

Mr. Robson pointed out to Jason that he felt this wasn't going to be straightforward delivery as the baby was breeching. It was a large baby, and they needed to turn the baby into a head down position.

It took a while before it was successful, and Emily was ready to push; she was wanting her baby out no matter how painful it was. She smothered herself with gas and air, as Frankie held her hand.

After six hours of pushing, the baby was finally out, and it was a boy. 8lb 8ozs. As the nurse took the baby to the trolley, he wasn't breathing! She stimulated the baby by rubbing its back, legs and arms. As she rubbed his back once more, he cried out! To her relief and to everyone else's.

Emily shouted out!

'My boy, give me my boy! Let me have my boy!
Colleen carried the baby to Emily as she cradled it with joy. At this point, everyone had tears in their eyes. It was an emotional moment as Jason and Mr. Robson stepped out of the room.

Mr. Robson spoke first,

'I am pleased that one is out of the way, it was getting a little tricky in there for a while. I think it's best we keep Emily under observation for this week in hospital. She has a weakened immune system and given her history of asthma it was the right decision to make'.

Jason fully agreed with him and said,

'That was an eye opener for me Simon, I applaud you for your expertise' Simon reciprocated the admiration by saying,

'You field of expertise of the head and brain; I couldn't contemplate such an idea'

As he smirked at Jason and raised an eyebrow.
Emily was exhausted and the nurse put the baby down in his cot with the other delivery babies.

Frankie too had his eyes almost closed as he lay his head on Emily's bed. Jacqueline left them to it as she made her way outside to Jason.

He put his arm around Jacqueline, and they made their way to the coffee lounge. He was ready for a well-earned coffee.

Jacqueline chatted and quizzed Jason about the delivery and he calmly replied,

'Everything will be fine, she did well, and it was hard work, but we all got there in the end'

Jacqueline was dying to know what name they had picked for the baby. She knew they picked two names they both loved, Callum or Daniel. Jacqueline liked them both.

As they made their way home, Jason dropped Jacqueline off at the cottage to be met by Colm and Bernadette and thereafter Niamh and Jack turned up.

They couldn't wait to hear the news! Niamh cried with joy!

'I will let her rest until tomorrow, but I am straight there at visiting time'

Jacqueline told her that was wise as she was so exhausted. How this day turned from pain and then into blissful woven joy.

A woven bliss, love like flickers into a tender kiss... as Jacqueline tenderly kisses her daughter on the cheek...

Chapter 19

The next day Emily awoke, she wasn't breathing well at all, her chest was making a rattling sound. Nurse Saunders quickly pressed the red button for immediate assistance.

It was not long before Mr. Robson was at Emily's bedside. He quickly ordered bloods to be taken as a matter of urgency.

As he examined her, he noted her breathing was becoming shallow, and she was given oxygen to revive her a little.

Moreover, he was worried about her left lung, as it didn't seem to be functioning well at all. Her temperature had risen once again, and the virus hadn't subsided. He tried to be diplomatic with Emily's questions so as not to alarm her. His suspicions were about her left lung which may have caused damage to her heart after such a problematic birth.

Mr. Robson acted quickly and rang for a cardiologist to attend promptly. Mr. Sampson who was the consultant on call, came along directly to Emily's bedside.

The blood test was back, and electrolytes, glucose, triglycerides, kidney and lung functions were not good.

Mr. Sampson would start her on a course of beta blockers and when she is stable, they would do a heart scan.

Within a matter of hours, it seemed her condition was stabilising a little but there was a long way to go.

The heart scan showed problems with the blood flow to one of the valves in her heart; the mitral valve which was causing the blood to flow backwards into the heart chamber. There was slight bulge there.

Emily was too weak for surgery, so it was a watch and wait for the moment. She would be monitored on a regular basis throughout the day.

Frankie was the first to be notified and he was inconsolable, he couldn't bring himself to go and visit his baby boy in the baby's room.

He called his best mate Ian who was out of town today on a job fixing a very expensive car, a jaguar.

'It's no good, I will have to call Jacqueline, or else, I will be in trouble', as he put his hands in his hair and rustled his fingers through the strands, up and down before he could bring himself to get up and reach for the telephone down the hall.

He dialled the number, and Jacqueline put the phone down without answering and rushed straight to the hospital. Frankie figured she would to that…. His hands were shaking. Mr. Sampson was the first to greet him on arrival and spoke out,

'Now lad, don't distress yourself, we have Emily stabilised, she is sleeping now.

You go and get some rest. It will be a few hours before she wakes up.

Frankie was going nowhere and waited for Jacqueline to arrive. She came running down the hallway, gasping for breath. Frankie put his hand up and said,

'She is asleep Jacqueline; we cannot disturb her for a few hours yet'.

Jacqueline was beginning to feel a little faint, as she slumped herself down at the nearest seat in the hallway and asked when she could see this Mr. Sampson. Frankie turned to her his face so drawn, and said,

'He has just left to go on his ward round; he will be back in an hour or so'.

A silent moment, as they both sat, not saying a word until Jacqueline suggested they go see the baby.

Frankie reluctantly spoke,

'You go; I will stay here just in case she wakes up. The nurse said she would let me know'

Jacqueline looked at Frankie, and wondered if he had been to see his baby boy? As she made her way to the baby's room the nurse directed her to her grandson. He lay so big and bonny with his eyes closed.

The nurse began telling Jacqueline how good he was.

'I expect the father will make an appearance before long', as she smiled back at Jacqueline.

'I am sure he will, said Jacqueline.

She was feeling a little doubtful on that score as she noted Frank's vacant expression when she asked him to come along with her. She would put it down to the shock of Emily being so poorly.

Emily was awake and Frankie was first in there as he held her hand and told her to not worry, as he tried to be positive…….

'You will be out of here before you know it love; it will be so good to get you back home. Emily tried to muster up a smile, but she felt something wasn't quite right inside her body.

Niamh arrived in the afternoon to see her dear sister. Frankie left the room to let Niamh, and her mam to have their time. Emily was glad to see them, but she was becoming frail and exhausted as she spoke quietly.

Jacqueline could see her daughter was becoming tired and as they were just about to leave, Emily asked her mam to stay behind for a moment.

She whispered in her ear,

'Look after my boy; please look after my boy' Jacqueline looked with concern and said to her daughter,

'I will pet for now, but you will be better soon, I know you will, see you tomorrow, get some rest'

They were all told to go home and get some rest….

Emily lay there as she could feel her heart giving way, and she felt the feeling of dread, and it wasn't going away….

The nightfall came with an alluring sound of the wind tapping on the hospital window, it was the long branches that had given way off the tree in the background...that tapped on the window... as the wind blew with vengeance...

Emily gave out a large gasp, as she clutched her left arm; the pain in her chest was shooting through her! She had suffered a cardiac arrest! And the crash team were violently trying to resuscitate her!

The CPR was not working, the adrenaline pumped into her was not working, the paddles did not revive her. They had to call it, after twenty mins in ….

Mr. Sampson, sadly spoke out reluctantly, 'It's time to you call it - Time of death, 2.30am!'.

She was gone! The team looked on with sadness... Nurse Saunders, put her hand on Mr. Sampson's shoulder and spoke,

'You did everything you could'.

He never liked losing his patients and he hadn't lost that many...

It was time to telephone Frankie, he didn't answer…. He was fast asleep in his bed…. Mr. Robson, the obstetrician, was informed and sat for a moment. He would make his way to the trauma ward as he knew Jason was on call.

As he walked through sliding doors, he caught sight of Jason... They both looked at one another and Jason knew what was coming….

Mr. Robson began by saying,

'I am sorry for your loss, they tried everything. It's a shame I was going to operate on her when she was strong enough to fix that leaky valve'...

Jason with tears in his eyes spoke out,

'I don't know how I am going to tell Jacqueline, I just don't, all I can do is to be there for her'

Mr. Robson informed Jason that they couldn't get hold of Frankie. He patted him on the back and left him to do the contacting.

Jason replied by saying,

'Frankie, poor lad he will probably be asleep'

It was now 5am, Jason called Jacqueline, and it was Niamh who answered the telephone.

He paused and Niamh prompted him with a matter of urgency,

'Jason, what has happened just tell me, tell me what has happened is it our Emily'

Jason began in a shaky voice,

'Yes, its Emily, I am so sorry Niamh, I am sorry, but we have lost her, she suffered a massive cardiac arrest, they tried so hard to save her'

Niamh at this point had dropped the phone and screamed out loud, 'Nooooooo! Not our Emily, Nooooooo!

Jacqueline came rushing down the stairs as she heard Niamh screaming and Colm too came out of his room brushing his hands against his eyes to get himself woken up!

'What is going on mam? What's with our Niamh screaming her head off.

As they both arrived at the bottom of stairs, Jacqueline could see the telephone off the hook, and she could hear a voice at the other end as she made her way towards Niamh! Who was on her knees with her hands all over her face.

Jacqueline picked the telephone up and Jason was still on the other end; she knew in her heart it was her Emily.

'It's our Emily, isn't it?'

Jason with tears in his eyes now, replied,

'Yes, my love, it is, I am so sorry for your loss', as he began telling her about what had occurred during the night.

She sat motionless by the telephone table just staring at the staircase, she listened to her Jason tell her that she no longer has her daughter anymore.

After a moment, she jumped up and said,

'I want to see her; I want to see her now'

Jason quickly responded, 'I will be with you, in ten minutes, my shift is nearly over, I will get the registrar to cover.'

First things first, I must call Father Donnelly, he must get there, she needs the last rites, she must have the last rites!

Father Donnelly was just getting out of bed, and he was devastated for them, and acted quickly he would be there before she was... he read the last rites to Emily... as he stood over her and blessed her before the anointment of the blessed oil. He couldn't believe it; he prayed for her soul to be delivered.

It didn't seem that long before Jason had arrived at Jacqueline's. She to comfort Niamh and Colm, and told Colm to look after his sister, as she left the house with Jason.

Mr. Sampson left Mr Robson to deliver the bad news to the rest of the family. He tried in vain to get through to Frankie and finally he answered the call. Frankie couldn't control his emotions he became too angry! He shouted down the phone to Mr. Robson... Mr Robson took his time and replied in a soft calm tone,

'I know this is not good news, and I am so sorry for your loss'

He tried in vain to get him to come to the hospital so they could talk further. Frankie wasn't going to go to the hospital, he didn't want to see Emily dead, he wanted to remember her alive!

Jacqueline walked down to where the morgue was situated which was down at the bottom of the hospital; the basement....

'How this corridor seeps of death!' she thought to herself... as she approached the room where they brought Emily out for her to view...

Her feelings were so alive for a moment, she thought she was in a dream... 'She is not dead, my Emily! She cannot be!

The moment they pulled the sheet away; she could see the white greyish face of death upon her! The realisation came flooding through, like the gushing of Niagara Falls!

Her emotions let loose! As she cried out! Jason quickly grabbed hold of her before she collapsed into his arms!

This night of sorrow was not going to end......... The pain seemed so sharp like someone had cut her in half....

Father Donnelly tried to comfort her the best way he could, but Jacqueline wanted to get back to her other children, she felt the urgency to get back! Jason was happy to get her back to her loved ones; it was going to be a raw night of pain for them all.

As they drove back, Jacqueline asked about Frankie? Jason informed her that Mr. Robson was going to telephone him once again. She was worried and spoke out,

'I will telephone him when I get in, I need to make sure he is alright too'

Jason looked at his wife to be and forgot for a moment how she cared about others before herself.... As he looked at her with pride...

The telephone rang out, but Frankie at this point had drunk half a bottle of whiskey by now....and was in no condition to answer the telephone.

Jacqueline would call it a night and call him first thing in the morning....

Chapter 20

Morning dew lay all around the sea front as Jacqueline threw open the bedroom window as she gasped for breath. It was once again upon her that feeling of loss.

'How can this be, how can my child go before me, that is not supposed to happen', as she talked incessantly to herself.

She had sent Jason home, in the night, that feeling of being alone with her own thoughts and feelings had pressed upon her heart and she made the excuse that Jason needed his sleep after a night on call.

It was time to stand up straight, get a grip as she went into the bathroom, still talking to herself.

'It's time to get Frankie to bond with his baby boy; the child only has one parent now, he must see sense, he must', she kept saying to herself.

Niamh appeared around her bedroom door; her eyes were red from crying. Jacqueline comforted her and spoke first.

'Come on my pet, you are stronger than this we must keep it together from Emily, she was so strong. She would want us to get organised, you know what she was like always forward planning'.

Niamh looked up at her mam, and smiled as she nodded,

'Your right mam, she would, let's go and see Frankie, see if we can knock some sense into him'

Colm came too, as he felt he might be able to persuade him to come to hospital to say goodbye to Emily and see his lovely baby boy.

They all arrived at Frankie's; his car was there so he must be in. He wasn't answering the door, they all went around the back and fortunately for them he hadn't locked the back door! Colm moved in first, no sign in the kitchen, as he opened the living room door, there was Frankie sprawled all over the settee with an empty whiskey bottle on the floor!

He lay snoring away, Colm prodded him in the back firmly, no answer. He went into the kitchen and filled a pan full of cold water and flung all over his head and face he screamed out,

'What the hell!'

As he opened his eyes there stood the three of them looking down at him. Colm shouted

'Come on Frankie, get yourself up and in the bathroom, get yourself washed and dressed you are coming with me to the hospital now!

Frankie stood up defiant!

'I am doing no such thing; you cannot make me. This is my house! Get out! of my house! Do you hear me!

Colm stood at loggerheads with him, toe to toe,

'What the hell has happened to you, where is your mind you stupid man! Your wife is dead! Your baby all alone! What kind of man are you! Not the one I used to know! That's for sure!

Frankie went to punch Colm, but his hangover was still upon him as he fell into Colm and began crying out loud!

'Leave me, leave me alone, I tell you, leave me alone!

Colm sat him back on the settee and Jacqueline began saying in a quiet tone, 'Come on Frankie son'

He was like a son to Jacqueline, and it was upsetting to see him like this. She further spoke,

'You just take your time and get dressed and we will wait, come on son, let's go to the hospital'

Frankie cried out in despair,

'I am sorry Jacqueline, I just cannot go, I just cannot, I won't!

Jacqueline got up and telephoned his parents Agnes and Gerald to come round immediately.

Gerald answered the telephone and was so shocked about the news. Jacqueline had no idea they hadn't been told, she thought Frankie would have informed them straightaway!

It didn't take them long as they both rushed into the living room. Gerald spoke to his son first.

'Come on lad, you are coming home with us for now, let's get you sorted lad, come on'.

Agnes hugged Jacqueline, as they both sobbed together at that moment. Colm put his arm on Jacqueline's shoulder and said,

'It's time to go home mam, come on'.

As they said their tearful goodbyes, Colm couldn't help but notice that Frankie was not in a good place at all. It is probably best to leave things for a few days. Gerald spoke to Jacqueline before getting into the car,

'Come round in a few days, I am sure we have lots to sort out' Colm agreed with him as they gave each other a manly hug.

The drive home seemed to take forever, as Colm was taking it slow, he couldn't get over Frankie's attitude, he believed him to be a strong, manly man, not a weak one… it didn't seem to fit well with him. He thought he loved his sister better than that… His anger seemed to come to the surface as he sped up a little….

Jacqueline shouted out,

'Don't go home Colm, let's go to the hospital to see baby Callum, he must be lonely on his own in that baby's room, he needs a cuddle'

Colm turned the car around and they made their way to the hospital. Nurse Chambers was on duty and greeted Jacqueline with a warm smile.

'Come on, I will take you to your Grandson, you can hold him if you like' Jacqueline smiled with joy, as she was so thankful!

As baby Callum was cradled into Jacqueline's arms, she looked down at him and said,

'You look like your Grandad Declan'

Niamh and Colm looked down at Callum, and Colm spoke

'I think you might be right, mam; he has his nose and chin'

Jacqueline was able to give him a feed, and she didn't want to leave him, but she knew she must. She asked if she could come along at his feed times in the day, and it was agreed that it would be a good thing.

Mr. Robson popped his head around and wanted to talk to Jacqueline about Callum, as he was fit and well and would need to be discharged into someone's care soon.

She stared at Mr. Robson as she answered abruptly,

'Someone's care! I will take care of him; he will come home with me'.

Colm butted in by saying,

'I will go back to Frankie's and fetch the cot mam from the baby's room. I will get Gerald to come and let me in'

Jacqueline quickly answered,

'Oh! Yes! That would be great son, bring plenty of baby's nappies and baby clothes. Oh! Don't forget the baby formula. Emily bought so much before she stopped herself saying anymore for fear of letting her emotions run away with her, this was not the time to fall apart....

Emily's body would remain in the morgue until such time they had organised the funeral arrangements.

Niamh felt that her dear sister should be put to rest now, it wasn't right she was stuck in that horrible morgue. She was going to give her sister the best send off, if Frankie didn't pull himself together.

It was time to bring baby Callum home, as Jacqueline cradled him in her arms, as she left the hospital.

Colm informed his mam that he would drop her off first and make his way to Gerald's to collect the key to Frankie's, he wouldn't be long.

Jacqueline spurted out,

'Take as much time as you like, I am quite happy having this lovely bonny lad on my lap'

Niamh smiled back and wanted her turn with Callum,

'Yes, I wouldn't mind having him on my lap either mam, when you are ready', as she gave her mam a cheeky smile.

For the first time, since Emily's death, they were all smiling, it was Callum, he brought some much joy in the house.

The telephone rang out, and Niamh got up to answer it, it was Jason on the other line. Jacqueline got up out of the armchair, and passed little Callum to Niamh,

'You can have your turn now', as she smiled at her daughter.

Jason asked if he could come round to see her, he was wide awake now. Jacqueline went on to say,

'I have baby Callum with me, Jason, I have my hands full! Why not come round later this evening, as I will be looking after Callum until things are sorted as Frankie has gone home with his parents'

It was a lot to take in for Jason, as he slumped on his telephone seat and spoke out,

"Oh, I thought Frankie would have taken the baby home with him and his parents would be looking after him?'

Jacqueline stood up with the phone in her hand with an annoying expression on her face before she answered.

'Well Jason, Frankie isn't well enough, and Agnes isn't in good health herself, so Mr. Robson and I had the conversation. I am more than happy to take care of my Grandson'

Jason quickly replied,

'I didn't mean it like that my love, I'm sure it will be sorted, it's only temporary, isn't it?'

Jacqueline couldn't believe her ears; Jason sounded a little selfish in her mind... She further went on to say to him,

'I don't know Jason, I am happy with any outcome if my grandson it well looked after, that what matters to me, it's important to me'

Jason said he would pop round about 7pm? If that was ok. Jacqueline answered snappishly,

'Yes, that's fine with me'

It was going to be a rather awkward evening he felt in his mind, he would have to step up to gain Jacqueline's affections, he felt she was slipping away, but on the other hand he felt it was early days, and he was sure she would be back to her usual self and they could get back to their wedding plans.....

Colm went into Emily's room; he felt her presence as he set up the cot. There were still some of Emily's things in the drawers. Her knitting patterns, and crocheted napkins

His eyes filled with tears as he wiped them away and quickly got on with the setting up of the cot.

He looked back and whispered as if Emily was still there, 'He is home sis; we will look after him for you'

Callum took to his bottle feeds; he was a hungry lad! and at 6pm he was put down in his cot, fast asleep.

Jacqueline stood over him, watching him as he slept. She too felt Emily's presence as she held one of the crocheted napkins to her mouth....

The doorbell rang and it was Jason....

Niamh greeted him at the door and shouted up to her mam... 'Jason is here mam'

She took her time and eventually entered the living room. She kissed Jason rather cooly....

Colm offered Jason a drink of Whiskey, he declined, he was on duty early the next morning.

A cup of tea was made, Colm and Niamh made themselves scarce. The awkwardness seemed to resonate around the room until eventually Jacqueline broke the silence.

'How are you, is everything good at work?' as she tried to divert the conversation away from anything personal.

Jason spoke in a warm tone of voice

'Oh, my love, I know this is a terrible time for you. I have not expressed myself properly. I know. I wonder if we could talk a little about our plans'

Jacqueline moved away from Jason and stood up to say!

'I don't know how you could be so selfish. Our plans! can wait and they will have to wait for some time'

Jason stood up and walked towards her,

'What do you mean for some time, how long is some time' Jacqueline went on to say,

'I think we should just leave it for now, I don't want to talk about it, I really don't. I think we should call it a night. I will show you out'

Jason was dumfounded as he made his way to the door… He went to kiss Jacqueline, and she gave him her cheek.

'I will call you tomorrow', as he walked down the path…….

Had he lost her, had he really lost her, he had a lot of thinking to do now….

Chapter 21

Frankie began pulling himself together at his parents' home, of which he was not too happy to be there. He tried in vain to persuade his dad to drive him home. The conversation got heated and Gerald began telling Frankie some home truths!

'Right lad, you sit back, don't say a word, and listen carefully. I am not going to repeat myself. This is how it is going to be; you are going to smarten yourself up and then we are going to the hospital so you can say your goodbyes to you wife!'

It took a moment for Frankie to digest what his father had said to him. He got out of the chair and up the stairs to get himself washed and dressed. He was still wearing his PJ's.

It took him awhile as he glanced in the mirror at himself and realised, he looked a sight! The realisation was starting to sink in, Emily was gone! And he cannot bring her back...

'I don't know if I can face this, I don't know if I can see her,' his thoughts kept going around his head. He would go with this father; he had no choice in the matter.... Their relationship was a good one and Frankie respected his father. He was going to try and get this over with....

His mam Agnes was crippled with arthritis and there was no way she would be able to go with them. Her health was deteriorating, and Gerald didn't want any more arguments in the household, he had told Frankie to mind his manners around his mam.

The drive seemed too short to Frankie, he just wanted to keep driving around, he would be happy with that... but that was not going to happen, and he knew it. His dad gave him a look of encouragement and in they went through the sliding doors into the hospital...

Mr. Robson was on duty, and he was happy to direct them to the morgue… The long walk down the corridor was getting too much for Frankie as he started to sweat profusely and his hands started to shake as he turned to his dad,

'I cannot do it Dad, I just cannot do it, you go say goodbye, please dad!'

Gerald took Frankie by the arm and noticed how ill he looked, and he knew then that he would have to get him some professional help, the shock and grief was too much for him, he could see that.

He sat him down on one of the seats along the corridor and put his arm around his son and began saying,

'It's alright lad, you just sit here for a few minutes, I will go get a nurse. He approached a nurse down the corridor who was very happy to sit with Frankie whilst his dad went to say goodbye to his daughter-in-law'

The nurse happened to be a psychiatric nurse, and her calming presence seemed to help Frankie in his hour of need.

Gerald went into the room where Emily lay, he kissed her on the cheek and whispered. 'Goodbye lovely lass, and Frankie is sorry, he says goodbye too'

His eyes filled with pain and tears as he took a moment to gather his thoughts…. He straightened his tie and put his shoulders back and took a deep breath and said to the morgue assistant.

'Thank you, I ready to go now'

The assistant escorted him out towards the corridor, where he was met by Nurse Lafferty, who spoke with him for a moment.

'Your son needs a referral to see a counsellor. Your GP can refer him, I would suggest you call him today'.

Gerald thanked the Nurse for her support and assistance. He made his way to Frankie, and they went off to the bistro by the seafront to get some fresh air.

Frankie was refreshed by the sea waves as they folded over so briskly cascading around the frothy fragments.

They sat on the deck of the bistro and Gerald went off to get them some coffee. Frankie began drifting with the waves, he was in a trance, and he liked that moment of not thinking or feeling anything, just the sea.... Its ambience calmed and relaxed him so...

As they sat with their coffee, Gerald began the conversation...

'Listen son, we need to get you some help, you need to see a counsellor lad, now don't get upset. It will help you, I know it will. I think I should take charge of the funeral arrangements with Jacqueline. I am going around to see her. I will get you home first lad.'

Frankie stared into the sea, it wasn't registering with him, and his father could see that. He would get Frankie the help he needs sooner rather than later.

They drank their coffee and Frankie seemed reluctant to move, but his father grabbed his arm and said,

'Come along son, let's get home'.

As they drove along, Frankie fell asleep... it must have been all that sea air in his lungs, as his father quickly glanced over to him...

They were home and Gerald prodded Frankie. Agnes looked a little distraught as she opened the door. Frankie went straight upstairs and into his bed and fell into a deep sleep.

Gerald explained to Agnes what had happened and told her not to worry about anything, he would sort everything out with Jacqueline. He kissed his wife tenderly and patted her shoulder.

'You get yourself in now pet, I will be back before you know it'

He then made his way to Jacqueline's and as he pulled up, he caught sight of Jason just getting out of his car.

They both nodded to one another and Jason knocked on the door… Niamh opened it and was surprised to see Gerald standing next to Jason.

'Come in you two, nice to see you both', as looked rather bemused.

Jacqueline was in the living room changing little Callum… as Gerald approached his eyes lit up...

'Oh, who is a bonny lad then, aye'.

Niamh asked them both if they cared for a cup of tea, they gladly accepted.

Jacqueline put little Callum down in the wooden cradle next to her chair as she put her two hands on her knees in anticipation of a tricky conversation with Gerald the grandfather.

Gerald began telling her about what had occurred at the hospital with Frankie, she sat back with a shocked but sympathetic expression on her face. She was overcome with surprise as she thought Frankie would be the tough cookie in all of this, but it was not the case.

Moreover, he began talking about the funeral arrangements with Jacqueline. He was aware that Emily was a Roman Catholic and wondered if Jacqueline would take care of the catholic service and he would take care of ordering the funeral cars.

Jacqueline sat back and was happy to do that, more than happy. She wanted her beloved Emily to have a proper Catholic burial which meant she would a Vigil Service the night before and her coffin would be brought into the Catholic church for the funeral mass and then onto the final burial interment at the cemetery.

Gerald took it all in and was glad Jacqueline was doing it; he hadn't a clue on any of it. They discussed the flowers and the coffin, which would be of fine oak. Jacqueline would sort that out too.

She would call Father Donnelly presently to arrange the date of service. Jason sat at the back just listening to him. He felt like an outsider and didn't know how he was going to approach Jacqueline. His thoughts were to give her a hand, but she may not want my hand, as he brushed his hair back with frustration....

The conversation turned to Callum, and Jacqueline hesitated for a moment and let Gerald speak first...

'I think it's best that you take care of little Callum Jacqueline, Agnes is in no fit state to look after him and Frankie, he is even worse. I don't think it's the right time to make long term commitments. I am hoping Frankie will turn himself around in a few weeks or so'

Jason's face changed, he was hoping Gerald was going to take little Callum... Jacqueline beamed with joy,

'Of course, I will look after my wee Grandson, Gerald. You and Agnes can visit as many times as you like. I do hope I see Frankie before long'.

He got up and walked towards Jacqueline and gave her a big hug and thanked her for doing this. He went onto to say,

'I must get back to Agnes; her arthritis isn't getting any better'

They said goodbye at the door, and as Jacqueline made her way back into the living room, she turned to Jason and said,

'I wasn't expecting you today, I thought you were going to telephone first' He looked a little sheepish, and answered quickly,

'I thought it was best to come around and clear the air, I think our conflicting views were a little muddled. I am so sorry, my love for what I said'

She sat next to little Callum as he slept... and spoke out

'It's alright dear, we know where we are now. I have lots of things to do as you just heard so I must get on'.

He stood up and asked if he could help in anyway...

'Thank you, you could ring the funeral Director for me and let him know about the Oak Coffin to be set aside until I arrange the date of service'

She felt she needed to let him do something as she didn't want to lose him completely... He smiled back at her knowing that he hadn't lost her forever.

I will leave you to it my love and get back with you later. Shall I order some tea in for us all? Would you like that.

Niamh was happy to hear it, and Jacqueline thought it was a nice gesture and wouldn't say no given all what they had to do on this busy day organising the funeral.

It took all the grief away from them when they were busy, they didn't have time to think too much about dear Emily.... Colm went straight back into work, and his Uncle Dylan supported him all the way...

Niamh went to little Callum as he woke up and Jacqueline was talking to Father Donnelly on the telephone, and he was happy to call round presently within the hour to sort out the funeral service with her... She was happy to hear his soothing voice on the other end of the telephone...

His calming presence in the living room helped the situation as they talked of hymns. Emily's favourite hymn was, 'Soul of my Saviour'.... The service was all sorted, including the Vigil Mass, and Father Donnelly went over to the wee lad, and patted him on the head as he spoke,

'I will see you soon wee boy, for your baptism'

Jacqueline was feeling a little weary with it all... as she left Callum a moment with Niamh as she put the kettle on and took a moment to think of her Emily… Her thoughts were to look after Callum indefinitely, as she couldn't see Frankie doing it alone… She would talk to him when the time was right….

Teatime had arrived and Jason didn't disappoint, he brought every meal under the sun, from Fish, steak, pasta, potatoes, relishes, apple pie, ice cream...

Jack came along too, he felt a little lonely himself as Niamh was supporting her mam, but he didn't mind, he loved her so, and wouldn't jeopardise their love for each other…for the sake of a few nights with her mam…

Colm and Bernadette had entered the room. The conversation turned to Frankie, and Colm would be the one to call on him in a few days, to see how he was doing.

The funeral was in five days' time on the Thursday… at 10.00am at St Bernadettes… After the meal was over. Niamh decided to go home with Jack, and Jacqueline agreed she should do that.

It wasn't long before the house was left with just Jacqueline Jason and baby Callum. The conversation seemed to dry up a little as they couldn't find the words…. It was Jacqueline who spoke out first…

'I think we should cancel the wedding for now, Jason, it's only a few months away. I feel it would be better to set a date next year, don't you'

Jason slumped back on the settee, alarmed and shocked, at such a suggestion, but couldn't find the words for fear of losing her. It was not what he wanted it all… instead he said quietly,

'If that is what you want my love, then we can talk again at a later date'

She thanked him and said she was having an early night as she was feeling a little tired. Little Callum will wake up in the night for a night feed.

He got up to wish her goodnight and tried to kiss her passionately, but Jacqueline seemed reluctant to participate, and a quick kiss was all he was getting.

As he got into his car, he felt that he was once again losing her little by little….

Chapter 22

Little Callum awoke, bang on time, 3am in the morning. He was a hungry baby; he so enjoyed his bottle of milk.

Jacqueline was beginning to think she will have to crush a few rusks, and put them in his bottle before long...

As she got him back to sleep, she sat awhile in the window seat and stared out at the stars. The moon was shining brightly... as she drifted into a poetic stance...

The moon its' congregation of aura
Its simmering glow... that over-flow... The wishing well is somewhere there... A romantic vision of love and care...

Jacqueline began to think of Jason and couldn't help feeling this doubt in her mind. There was a distance between them now, and it was little Callum. As she looked back at him sleeping...

She had made her mind up now, if Jason cannot accept Callum as a part of their lives in the permanent sense, then there was no point in continuing...

It would be up to him to make this commitment, and if he felt he couldn't then they would part ways.

She would have that conversation with him later that day, as she yawned. 'I must get some shut eye', as she whispered to herself...

It was going to be a busy day, organising the funeral, as there wasn't much time left as she lay in her bed.

Niamh awoke at 6am and could hear Callum crying... She went into Emily's bedroom and picked him up, but he was resolved in his crying moment.

She began to panic a little, as she tried to hush him by rocking him side to side, it wasn't working.

'Oh, my goodness, would I be cut out for this sort of thing? It looks like hard work to me, as she mumbled out loud.

Jacqueline came into the bedroom and spoke

'Oh, what is all the fuss about my wee bairn… come to nana'

As Niamh handed him over, he stopped crying instantly. She turned to her mam, 'How does that happen? I don't think I am maternal at all'

Jacqueline laughed out loud as she looked at Niamh...

'Aww pet, it just comes naturally; you just wait and see when you have one of your own. Trust me, I know what I am talking about.

Niamh was not convinced at all at such a notion… She felt a little uneasy with the mention of her having one of her own….

After his feed, Jacqueline bathed him and changed his nappy. Callum was quite happy and content now, as looked up at Jacqueline, gurgling… away…

Niamh looked on and could see how they had both bonded, like a mother and baby… only she wasn't the mother…. She looked a little concerned as she felt that it may cause problems later… when Frankie came to take his son home…

Her thoughts turned to Frankie, and she would have a word with Colm to see if they could both go and visit him to see how he was doing. She was eager to see how the land lied…

In the meantime, Jason had telephoned the funeral Director and sorted his part in assisting with the funeral arrangements. He was keen to get to Jacqueline's and didn't telephone. He just turned up at the door.

Colm answered the door and greeted Jason in his friendly manner. He liked him a lot. He showed him into the living room and shouted at the bottom of the stairs to Jacqueline.

Niamh looked at her mam and spoke out. 'Mam, Colm is shouting, Jason is here'

Jacqueline took a moment before answering.

'I will be down in a few minutes, you go down' Niamh gave her mam a staring look, as if to say,

'It's you he has come to see, not me!'

She went down the stairs and smiled at Jason and offered him a cup of tea before saying,

'Mam will be down shortly'.

Jason looked a little dismayed at such a statement. He knew very well where she was and felt it would be some time before she entered the room. In fact, it was fifteen minutes later.

He got up and greeted Jacqueline with a peck on the cheek, he wasn't going for a full- on kiss, not in front of the children.

The conversation got off to a good start, as he informed Jacqueline he had telephoned the Funeral Directors.

They began talking about the Funeral Service Program to be distributed to all friends and family. Niamh had taken care of that because Jacqueline was so consumed with Callum. She barely let him out of her sight.

Everything was arranged and Niamh got up to suggest that her mam and Jason take a turn around the sea front, as she looked at her mam and spoke decisively,

'Mam, you need to get out of the house and have some time with Jason, it will do you good'

Jason was pleased with that outburst; it took a moment before Jacqueline gave in and agreed to a walkabout on the sea front.

It was a bit chilly, and windy. The sea looked rather choppy... so she put on her duffle coat and hat.

As they sauntered slowly along the seafront and watched those brave surfers still going out on such a day.

Jason took hold of Jacqueline's hand, and hoped it would be gratefully received, and it was to his relief.

He began saying that he didn't mind about the delay with their marriage plans and he was happy to be there for her.

She held his hand tightly and was happy that he had said these words, and she now felt it would be much easier to get him on board when she has permanent custody of Callum….

They had the most relaxing time, and Jacqueline had to admit she had been missing him. Her mind turned to Callum as she turned to Jason to say,

'I must get back, Jason, Niamh was in a panic this morning when he awoke, I don't want to leave him too long'

He turned away from her as he stared into the sea, feeling a little disappointed, but quickly smiled back at her as he felt he had made baby steps in getting her to spend more time with him.

It wasn't going to be easy, but he was determined to win her back, as his thoughts were that Frankie would eventually want Callum with him…

As they entered the cottage, Niamh was pleased to see her mam as Callum had just woken up, and she was ready to go and see Frankie.

Jacqueline thought it best to leave him be, but Colm insisted that they were both going for a visit that was all…

Niamh began the conversation in the car with her brother and conveyed her concerns about how Jacqueline was attached to Callum. Colm thought it was good for the baby to bond with his grandmother, as he hasn't been an ounce of bother with her. He thought the baby would have missed its mother.

Mixed emotions from them both, but it was now time to see Frankie. Gerald opened the door, and he was pleased to see them both.

He let them know that Frankie had seen the counsellor, and he will be seeing a Mr Cumberland, for the next 6 months.

Colm and Niamh were happy to hear it, and he looked a little better than last time they saw him.

Niamh couldn't wait to talk about Callum, but Frankie looked rather uncomfortable when Callum was mentioned, it just reminded him of Emily, and he didn't want to go there not now.

Colm could see his despair in his eyes, and stopped Niamh in her tracks as he said, 'Well, you should all come and visit soon, for tea'

Gerald and Agnes were keen on seeing the baby and as Gerald saw them to the door, he said to Colm,

'I will get him to visit soon, he is doing alright, but best not push it just yet' As they both got into the car, Colm spoke out first,

'Callum is settled our Niamh, even you can see that'

Niamh looked a little surprised at his comments, but she couldn't help thinking he was right, but she worried about the long-term future... In her mind, Callum should be bonding with his dad...

The week progressed in a sombre manner, as the vigil mass was upon them all. Jacqueline took Callum along to see his mother, although he wouldn't know anything about it, but it soothes her heart to have him in her arms and talk to him about her.

Gerald and Agnes were not having the best time trying to persuade Frankie to attend the Vigil mass...

His father put his foot down and eventually got him in the car....

Frankie had taken his medication and was feeling a little calm and just wanted it to be over with.

Father Donnelly had prepared the service and homily, and they would say the rosary in memory of Emily... in readiness for the Funeral Service tomorrow.

Emily lay in front of the altar as Jacqueline entered the church with Callum in her arms and Jason by her side.

Niamh and Jack followed on with Colm and Bernadette. Jacqueline's sisters Sara and Aileen attended along with Serena and Dylan. They had left the twins with her parents.

As Frankie entered the church with his father, he pulled away quickly as he saw the coffin and he stared at the baby… he shouted…

'I cannot do this! I won't do it!'

He ran out of the church, as Father Donnelly looked on, and took a moment to gather everyone…

Gerald immediately followed his son out, Agnes behind him. They found Frankie on the grass sobbing and shaking… It was time to take him home.

Agnes turned to her son and said,

'You don't have to do anything my son, you just need to get better son, don't worry we will get you better', as she cradled her son….

The service began and it was a beautiful service as they sang 'Ave Maria, gratia plena' which is 'Hail Mary Full of Grace'

Jacqueline loved that hymn, it brought her so much comfort. Jason squeezed her hand, and she squeezed his back.

It was going to be a trying time, and Father Donnelly came to offer his support, and he would visit Frankie when the time was right.

The Funeral Mass the next day was emotional and the absence of Frankie and his mam was noticed.

Gerald went over to see Jacqueline and Jason with baby Callum and had the conversation. It was thought that Jacqueline should take full custody of Callum and in time maybe Frankie will want to see his son, but Gerald was doubtful on the subject for at least the next 6 months, until his treatment was fully completed.

Maybe then he might start to recover fully and want his son back.

Jacqueline looked on and was happy to have Callum longer, she didn't want to speak about permanency at this stage, but she felt that Callum would be well settled with her…by then….

Jason however, was thinking on the lines of in 6 months' time would he be able to get the wedding plans back of track??

Chapter 23

The aftermath of Emily's funeral had taken its toll on poor Niamh. The realisation that she would not be seeing her sister again had just hit home with her.

Jack could feel her pain and knew she would be grief stricken after the funeral, as she had been holding herself together...

He decided that he would go down to the travel agent and book a holiday.

'I know just the place to take her, the Lake District, that is where all the famous poets used to hang out, she will love it'.

The timing was right, there was a lovely cottage to rent for a week, and he booked it there and then, no hesitation... First things, first, I must call Patrick, his Senior Manager to get the week off, he owed him, as he had been working around the clock at the pit for weeks. Patrick told him to have two weeks off; he had earned it...

Niamh was on compassionate leave, and it was ideal, he thought to himself. She was at her mams; he couldn't get there quick enough to give Niamh the good news.

When he arrived at Jacqueline's his Uncle Dylan was there to support Niamh, as she was his favourite niece.

It was Dylan who opened the door to Jack, and he was pleased to see him, they both stood in the hallway and chatted for moment.

Dylan was happy to hear about the holiday news and thought it was an excellent idea. He prompted Jack to go into the living room and gave Niamh the good news...

She didn't answer at first and Jack was feeling a little apprehensive at her long pause before she answered......

'I think that is a wonderful thing you have done my pet', as she cried on his shoulder.

Jack held her face in his hand and said softly,

'You are precious to me, my pet, and I know you will find some joy with all those places to visit like Kirkstone Foot, at Ambleside. Your favourite poet Keats visited there my love. That is where we are staying in a cottage nearby'

They held each other as Dylan and Jacqueline made themselves scarce and entered the kitchen.

'Time for a cuppa I think, don't you Dylan' as she winked at Dylan.

He replied with a sly wink of approval back at Jacqueline.

The conversation turned to the wee bairn Callum, Jacqueline explained the situation to Dylan, and he asked if Jason was alright with that.

She turned to Dylan with a sharp reply,

'Well, it is my decision, and if he isn't alright about it then our relationship is in trouble. He hasn't said he isn't alright about it, so I assume we are doing okay.

She quickly changed the subject to the twins and Dylan had a wide smile on his face as he began telling her how they are growing so fast. Amy is walking around the furniture well now and has taken her first few steps on her own!

Whilst Ethan is crawling madly along to catch her up, I don't think he will be long, as he crouched by the settee last night and pulled himself up for a minute. I think it was a little shock to his system as he plunged down on his backside and screamed with frustration! Serena and I were laughing so loud, he put his hand up to us, as if to say,

'Stop that! I want to get up! Jacqueline laughed as she spoke,

'Aww the bonny bairns, I think it's time I took Callum around to visit, don't you'

Dylan was more than pleased with that response. He was noticing how Callum had captivated her life and how she was preoccupied with him. It kept her away from her grief...

They both went through to the living room to join Niamh and Jack and as they did so, Colm and Bernadette appeared at the door.

It was lovely get-together, but Dylan had to say his goodbyes and get back to his family. He opened the front door to say goodbye to Jacqueline.

As he was making his way to his car, he caught sight of Jason just making his way to the gate. He got out of the car to greet him.

Jason looked at little forlorn Dylan thought and asked him how things were going. He shook head and said,

'Well, the wedding is delayed until Frankie's recovery, which will be in 6 months they are hoping, but Jacqueline doesn't want to set a date yet? I am hoping things will settle down. My main concern is she is getting too attached to Callum'

Dylan told him not to worry too much about it, as he confidently said,

'These things have a way of sorting themselves out in the long run'

He didn't seem that convinced himself, as he thought it was a tall order for Frankie to take care of his son alone, given his mam is so ill.

Jason entered the cottage and could see she had company, he was hoping he could have Jacqueline alone to see if he could persuade her to set a date for the wedding. He would bide his time.

Bernadette was engrossed with little Frankie as she sat on the floor next to his cradle. She was a natural, as she cooed and whispered at the wee bairn,

'Oooh who is this bonny little lad then, aww, he got a lovely smile, haven't you now',

Jacqueline pointed out it was probably wind as he was only a few weeks old, she seemed a little reluctant to let Bernadette hold him but gave in to the matter as Colm went to pick him up.

It looked like Colm and Bernadette were happy giving Callum all the attention as they sat in the alcove by the bay window.

Jason beckoned Jacqueline to the kitchen and said,

Let's have some quiet time together shall we, in the kitchen'

She paused and didn't really want to, she wanted to keep an eye on Callum, but Colm prodded her,

'You go with Jason mam; we are happy here'

As they sat at the table, she asked if he would like a drink. For the first time, Jason said,

'Yes, I will have glass of red wine, will you join me'

She was surprised, but he pointed out to her he wasn't on duty for 36 hours, so would gladly like a glass of red wine. He was hoping this would loosen her up a little as she seemed so consumed with Callum and uptight when they were together…

He poured out two glasses put the bottle on the table, hoping she would take another… The conversation was a bit slow at first, but as she relaxed a little bit, they began talking about themselves.

Jason spoke about them going out one night, like a date night. She didn't seem to dislike the idea, and for the first time Jason was feeling upbeat and excited about it. He would book the mantra room at the pavilion on the sea front as the restaurant overlooked Marsden Bay… It was romantic...

Colm and Bernadette were thrilled with the news, they would baby sit of course, they would be delighted…

Jacqueline was surprised by their enthusiasm and the look on her son's face, said it all. She would go out just this once....

The date night came around swiftly, and Jason was finally going to get a whole evening with Jacqueline on her own.

He had ordered Champagne on arrival. The Mantra was the place to go for the finest cuisine; the steaks were unbelievable at this establishment.

Jacqueline had made such an effort and put on her best dress, a floral pastel design which complimented her figure.

Colm was startled by her appearance as she came down the stairs and remarked on it,

'Wow mam, you look sensational, Jason will be overwhelmed, I bet' As he arrived, he was certainly overwhelmed and said so....

'You look a million dollars, my love, all the men in the restaurant will be so jealous'

She had to respond to Jason and her son,

'All right now, that is enough of that, shall we go'

Jacqueline repeated to Colm and Bernadette on what to do with the bottles of milk, 'He won't need a feed for a few hours; I have changed his nappy'

Colm shouted out to her,

'We got it mam; you get off now'

The Mantra restaurant was illuminating, and Jacqueline was enjoying her date night, and the food was delicious.

After a few hours though she was itching to get back, she was hoping they weren't coping well.

Finally, Jason gave in and booked the taxi back to the cottage, he was staying the night, so it wasn't that bad...

As they arrived back at the cottage, Jacqueline was a little disappointed that Callum had settled and they had both done a great job.

The passionate night Jason was hoping for didn't go according to plan as Jacqueline didn't seem to connect with him at all….

As they lay, she couldn't bring herself to fully commit to Jason as she was worried, she wouldn't hear Callum if he needed her.

She said she was sorry, but it wasn't the right thing to do for her this night, but they should just lie together...

Jason stayed awake all night, and it was 3am on the dot Callum woke up and he got up, but Jacqueline pulled him back and said,

'You sleep; I will see to him' He lay, his mind thinking,

'Is this really going to work, it doesn't look like it to me'

His doubts started to creep in bit by bit as the night unfolded….

Chapter 24

Aileen arrived at Jacqueline's the next morning to talk about the ownership of the shops now Emily had passed. There was a clause in the Transfer that stated if Emily dies before her mother, then the ownership would go to her. Emily had decided to put her mam's name forward as Frankie had no dealings or interest in the shops.

It did stipulate however that any profits would go to Frankie. She felt her mam was the ideal candidate to take over, as her sister Aileen hadn't got the time to deal with them anymore. She was too busy with her husband Arthur and his string of companies...

Jacqueline had forgotten all about the shops and felt that Belinda would be taking care of them. Little did she know that Belinda was overwhelmed with it all and needed help and support... She had telephoned Frankie a few times, but he never answered...

As they both sat and discussed the future of the shops, it was suggested that Aileen go and see Belinda to see how the land lies.

Baby Callum was in Jacqueline's arms as usual, and Aileen asked her to put the baby down so they could talk properly. Jacqueline didn't seem to want to, but Aileen insisted...

'Now, let's talk this through, I know Serena has a great interest in the haberdashery shop, but she is probably too busy with the twins. Also, her mam is a good artist, we should approach Charlotte first to get her views. I think we should bring another assistant on board. Belinda only has Jenny... and young Olivia... What do you think Jacques?'

Jacqueline didn't seem to mind at all, her mind was firmly fixed on Callum, she just nodded, yes'.

Aileen got up and replied... to that...

'Can I just say this, you are far too attached to this wee bairn, you have your own life with Jason, and what about the wedding?'

Jacqueline stoned faced at this point, raised her voice to say,

'Well, sister, you wouldn't have clue would you about babies, because you have never had any'

Her sister gave her a stark firm look in the eye before she answered,

'Thank you for reminding me, not that I ever wanted children, that's not the point, it was how it was said! And on that note! I wish you goodbye', as she stormed out of the house and into her car.

She sat in the car, and couldn't recognise her own sister, they had never had words like that ever. Aileen was worried about her sister, and she had caused to be…

Jacqueline sat still as a statue, she too, couldn't understand why she had said those horrible words to her sister, she was mortified at her change of character and would apologise when she next saw her.

She started to question herself as she repeated the words her sister had said to her and thought out loud,

'Maybe she is right, maybe I have consumed myself in Callum's world and shut everybody out, I must do something about that'

She hoped Frankie was getting better… and thought about calling on him in a few days to see how he was doing...

Father Donnelly was at Gerald's home to see Frankie, Gerald and Agnes left them to it…. Frankie liked Father Donnelly and began telling him of his fears for the future……. The words of wisdom came flooding out of Father Donnelly's mouth as he spoke,

'Grief is not an illness lad, it is a way of life, you just take it step by step and find comfort in the things that soothe you...

The pain never goes away, but it does dull as time passes. Seek out your kind of calm.... May I suggest just sitting in my church all alone... when there is no mass to attend... and have a spiritual experience with God. I am not saying it is your cup of tea, but you may find that calming, peaceful sense that you so yearn for'...

Frankie listened with the longing of such peace.... He would try it out; that feeling that spiritual need was consuming him as he sat with Father Donnelly....

Gerald and Agnes noticed Frankie was a lot calmer when Father Donnelly left... they thought it would be a great idea. They would all go to the church later that day....

It was an enlightening experience for all of them as they sat in church... no one was present just the three of them... Frankie stared at our Lady's statue and lit a candle; he felt her eyes upon him. His thoughts were, 'hasn't she got kind eyes'

He reflected on his marriage to Emily right here at this altar and his pain was sitting with him, but the spiritual existence Father Donnelly's was talking of was also within in. It was giving him some kind courage... He felt a strength he hadn't felt before; he wasn't caving into his grief.

As they left the church, Frankie turned to his dad, and said, 'Take me to Emily's grave dad, I want to talk to her'

Gerald turned to his son and answered,

'I certainly will lad; she will be glad to see you'

Agnes and Gerald stayed behind Frankie and left him alone with Emily. As he stooped down at the grave and placed some daisies upon it, he began his speech to Emily.

'I am so sorry my pet, I have been such a weakling, such an idiot. I fear I have let you down my dearest love, but not anymore. I need to put things right, I need to go and see our son, I need to look after him... I don't know how... but I think your mam will help me.'

He felt her presence upon him her smile of agreement, he could almost visualise her real being next to him, it was the most satisfying thing he had felt since her death....

Gerald and Agnes at this point were feeling so happy that Frankie had turned the corner for they feared he would never return to his old self...

It was agreed; they would go and see Callum.... Frankie was a little nervous, but he couldn't wait to hold his little boy for the first time....

As Jacqueline opened the front door, she was stunned at the presence of Frankie standing next to her.

'Oh, my dear boy! Come in! come in! You too Gerald and Agnes'

Callum lay in his cradle, his eyes were open as Frankie approached and said to Jacqueline,

'Can I pick him up' She replied,

'Of course you can, he is your son, be careful now, cradle his head, we don't want it drooping'

Frankie put his hand under his head and cradled him in is arms as Callum looked up as his dad.... It was a moment of pure joy for them both, as Frankie began talking to his son

'Hello there, little fellow, this is dad, here, I have come to look after you' Jacqueline looked on with a little fear in her eyes...

They sat down, and Frankie began putting out a plan of action... on how to take care of Callum long term...

He began saying to Jacqueline, that would she mind looking after him during the day when he was at work.... Would that be alright with her.

She looked relieved that she wasn't losing Callum altogether. In her opinion, he was a great plan. Frankie could drop him off in the mornings, and if he had to work late, she could have him overnight on occasion. They could work around each other....

Frankie was on sick leave and wondered if he could have Callum for now, until he returns to work in a week or so....

Jacqueline thought that was a good idea...

'I think it's time for tea and cake, don't you' as she looked at Gerald and Agnes.

They both agreed that would be wonderful... Frankie gave Callum to his mam, and followed Jacqueline into the kitchen...

He told her all about Father Donnelly, and she was so pleased everything had turned out well. They both talked of Emily and this short-term rift between them had completely disappeared as she hugged her son-in-law so tightly, she almost squeezed him to death.

Jacqueline began going through Callum's schedule and showed him how to fill baby's bottles with milk. He watched her so closely, so he wouldn't forget...

'Now, for the tricky bit, let's go and change his nappy' Frankie was nervous about this, and as Jacqueline showed him, she unpinned the nappy and let him have a go. It was on the third attempt he had down to a tee...

She gathered all his belongings and Gerald took the cot out of the bedroom but left the cradle in the living room for Jacqueline.

It was time for them to say goodbye for now.... As Jacqueline kissed them all, and held her grandson for a moment... She then passed him to his father.

As they left the cottage, Jacqueline shut the door and sighed.... A moment later, she cried incessantly.... And then she calmed herself and called Father Donnelly. It was his spiritual guidance she needed at that point, and he came around to see her immediately and put her mind at rest and at ease. He spoke with such compassion ...

'Now it's your turn to put your happiness first, just this once, my girl...' The pain now will be the joy you experience later...It's God's way to make you understand, It's the way of life... but it doesn't have to be pain forever, for there is so much joy to be had thereafter'

Jacqueline felt the sense of peace she always felt with her faith. She was now feeling a sense of guilt because she hadn't treated Jason properly at all, and he was being very patient. She must now put that right....

As Father Donnelly left her, she picked up the telephone and called Jason, he was so surprised to hear from her so soon, and even more surprised when she told him to come around as soon as he could.... He didn't hesitate and put the telephone down and made his way to her...

As he arrived Jacqueline smothered him with kisses, he couldn't get his breath... 'Who is this wonderful woman in front of me, where has she been'

Jacqueline relayed the whole happenings of the day to him, and he was relieved and elated at the same time.

The moment of truth was upon him. He got down on one knee, and once again proposed to her... and added,

'Let's get married as planned, I know it's only a month away, but we could still do it, what do you think'

She raised him up and whispered in his ear... 'Yes, I do'

Chapter 25

Aileen began preparation for a new assistant to join the haberdashery shop. Her journey was taking such a long time, as the roadworks were along the Sunderland Road... She was fifteen minutes away from South Shields.

'Let's hope there is parking spaces... oh why did I pick such a spot to buy a Haberdashery shop, seems so long ago now...1956... How I wish Emily was still here, it was a great day when I handed the shop over to her in 1969 as she thought out loud....'

Finally, she was moving along ... Belinda was looking out for her and saved a parking space by putting one of the shop's parking cones next to her car. Aileen was relieved to see it...

They went inside the shop to discuss the advertisement for new staff, and it was agreed they would both interview the ideal candidates.

Belinda suggested it wouldn't be a bad idea to recruit two candidates, one being a male as there would be heavy lifting involved in the art gallery ....

Moreover, it would be ideal when the deliveries arrived, as the boxes were so heavy... That gave Aileen an idea, she thought that in the long term they may be able to deliver straight to the door for special customers at least... or those who were indisposed. As she spoke out,

'Right, we will advertise for two candidates, one for a salesperson and one for a handyman, ideally with a driver's licence.'

The inventory of incoming and outgoing was well up to date, as dear Emily was stickler for keeping the books well balanced. Belinda looked at Aileen before she made another suggestion...

'It would probably be a good idea to pick someone who is familiar with bookkeeping. I think we are looking for a methodical person, a stickler like Emily'

The morning had turned out rather well, and Belinda was feeling that much easier, she could now breathe a little...

As Aileen sat having her cup tea in the back room, she contemplated on whether she would visit her sister to see how the land lay... She couldn't leave it like that, not after that terrible argument... It had played on her mind all night.

She got up and got into her car and before she knew it, she was knocking on Jacqueline's door.

As the door opened, Jacqueline grabbed her sister and put her arms around her before saying...

'Oh, our Aileen, come in pet, I have so much to tell you'

Aileen was relieved at such a reception and was curious about all the news. They both went into the kitchen to sit down ...

Jacqueline started the conversation by saying,

'Firstly, I want to say I am so sorry Sis, I don't know what came over me, forgive me'

Aileen forgave her quickly, as she was eager to know all the news. Jacqueline began...

'Frankie has taken little Callum; he is so much better than we could hope for. I will look after Callum when he is at work. Finally, sis, you will be pleased with what I am about say.... 'Jason and I are getting married as planned on the 4 November'

Aileen got up out of her chair and raised her hands,

'Hallelujah! Amen to that!', as she went over to kiss her sister...

She enquired about Niamh and Jack and wondered how they were getting on. Jacqueline hadn't heard from them, so she was hoping it was all going well... at the Lake District.

Niamh and Jack were having the most glorious time as they sauntered around the breathtaking views of the lakes... Their walks would take them to the dramatic fells and the waterfalls. Those mountains; a sight to see... It was so romantic, as it was beginning to feel like a second honeymoon.

They were both in raptures of such an idyllic landscape that had everything... Historic villages, such as Grasmere, Wordsworth the famous poet lived there... Quite a few of the romantic poets had ventured in the paths they had walked. It felt so surreal for Niamh.

Jack was quite surprised at how he loved the landscape, not to mention the ancient Castlerigg Stone Circle. That profound connection to History. He was quite consumed with it all...

The tranquillity surrounding the lakes, seem to be doing Niamh so much good and she even had rosy cheeks in the process...

As they left the waterfalls, they made their way to the lovely country inn to have a bite to eat... It had that rustic feeling, with his coal fire burning away. The dark mahogany wood beams and furniture seem to give it that Elizabethan effect that kept the history alive...

It was rather cosy... but their cottage was even cosier, that country feel about it. They would go the local village and gather some food essentials for the evening meal... after they afternoon at the Inn.

Jack was looking forward to that as it had a lot of farm shops which smelt so delicious as they walked into them...

Homemade food, Bread, cheese, chutney, pickle. The meat section was wholesome, such fresh beef, pork, sausage lamb, chicken...

They had bought a lot of produce, it looked like Niamh would be cooking a beef dinner, just like her mam would.

She hoped it would taste as good, but she was quite confident in the kitchen…. Her mam had taught her well…

The cake shop was divine, Jack was straight in there, he loved a Chocolate Fudge Cake… Niamh, preferred the lemon drizzle cake...

As they made their way into the kitchen, Jack said that he would help Niamh prepare, that's all he could do though. He was old fashioned like his dad, as his mam did all the cooking….

As they stood laughing and chatting as they chopped up the ingredients, Niamh bantered with her husband and said,

'Here there is a spare pinny my pet'

Jack snared at his wife and sarcastically replied to that comment,

'Not in your life, hinny. I am here to do a bit of chopping, then I am off outside to take in this beautiful view we have of the lake… I will leave you to it once I have chopped these vegetables up', as he winked back at her… and grabbed a bottle beer in the process...

Niamh got herself organised and even wrote down a few tips her mam had taught her… Meat, beef dripping, slow cook in the oven for a few hours. She had her, Oxo's gravy salt and flour in readiness for the gravy…later…

Now, Yorkshire pudding mix, plain flour, 2 eggs, salt, water, milk. I will do my mam's method, pour in the flour, add the tablespoons of water mix in and add the milk beat until smooth until air bubbles surface, add the two eggs, hand whisk the mixture until air bubbles are in full flow. Leave aside until ready to pour in the Yorkshire pudding tray…

The meat had been in the oven now for ninety minutes, as she pulled it out to baste the beef dripping… She poured some of the beef dripping into the Yorkshire pudding trays and lay them underneath in the oven... to sizzle, then she would take out the meat as it was tender but needed a little more cooking, she gave the meat a final basting.

The meat was ready to take out after a further ten minutes of cooking, and the Yorkshire pudding trays were sizzling. She gave her Yorkshire pudding mix a final whisk and poured them in the oven for twenty-five minutes. She had the potatoes and vegetables on a low heat... so everything would come together she thought, fingers crossed.

Five minutes before placing everything on the plates she would make the gravy.... The meat essence was fabulous, makings of great gravy, such a beautiful smell the aroma was making her so hungry. It was time to plate up, and the Yorkshire puddings rose so high with all those air bubbles she was one happy lady... as she beamed with joy...

Jack entered through the front door and shouted...

'My Oh! My! what a glorious smell, looks like a glorious dinner is about to be eaten'

He was not disappointed it was a great dinner; it was all down to the fresh produce... Niamh began saying,

'It's so good to eat, farm fresh food, nothing like it'.

Jack opened a bottle of red wine and began saying to his wife,

'You know what my love, we should make this place our favourite place to visit at least once a year'

Niamh smiled back at her husband as they sipped her red wine and couldn't agree more. They took their deserts outside to admire the view and took a further bottle of red wine.

The stars began to fall, they hadn't realised they had sat out so long with the blankets on their knees... Jack got up and carried his wife to the bedroom...

Niamh spoke,

'This is like a honeymoon; it is a place for a honeymoon'

They lay in a passionate embrace and Jack was so overcome with his passion he forgot to take precautions. He asked Niamh, but she was so consumed with the passion she told him not to stop....

The night was filled with such passion and love; it was a night to remember. It took away any anguish or regret.

Furthermore, it took away the grief for a while... Jack was so happy to see his wife looking so serene and radiant as he lay in the bed looking across at her...

She murmured and opened her eyes, she put her arm around Jack and said, 'I don't think we have had such a night... I love you so much'

Jack kissed his wife and answered,

'We didn't take any precautions! My pet, how do feel about that' She murmured,

'I feel absolutely marvellous, I don't care that we didn't take precautions, he was so perfect my love, so beautiful'.

He lay astounded, as he thought that Niamh may regret it, as she loved teaching and they hadn't really had a long conversation about babies.... He was happy if she was happy... That is all Jack cared about...

The week of woven bliss that came together... those threads of love that flowed and flowed... like a river... no more the shiver....

It was a week to remember, and they didn't really want it to end, but it was time to say goodbye to the Lake District for now.

They headed home to their cosy apartment in South Shields, as they drove along the coastline. Jack remarked on the Lake District being their second favourite place to be, but Sandhaven Beach was their perfect place... It was home...

Chapter 26

It was a cold and misty morning, it was now October, and the leaves began to flow on the grassy lawn outside Gerald and Agne's home.

Gerald liked the Autumn; he loved the glow of the rustic leaves he felt it resembled a new light, a new season, it had a kind of warmth about it, even though it was rather chilly.

Callum was full of voice this early morning, 6am. He had been unsettled, and Frankie was finding it rather challenging looking after this son, but he was determined. He felt Emily on his shoulder, and he didn't want to disappoint her memory.

He jumped out of bed and went into his son and picked him up and began having a conversation with him.

'You know my wee bairn, you don't have to make that much noise, I am here, we will get used to one another, your mama is here too, in spirit. She was the best there ever was. A beautiful creature to look at, just like you, my boy. You have your mama's eyes'

Callum looked up at his dad watching his mouth go up and down and then he stopped crying. He just stared at his dad.

Frankie looked down at his son and whispered...

'Right my little one, let's get you fed, bathed and dressed. Then we can go for a little outing... It might take a little while, as you know I am not that great with the nappy changing. So, if you stop wriggling about, then we can go down to the beach... I know you would like that'

He looked down at this son gurgling away and believed his son understood every word he had said to him.

He seemed to work because the nappy went on him first time... Frankie said out loud with confidence.

'I knew you were listening to me; I know you now, by wee bairn', as he kissed him on the cheek...

Agnes looked in to see how her son and grandson were doing. She didn't look at well, the arthritis was taking its toll, but she was so happy to see her son and Grandson bonding so well.

Frankie spoke with this mam and told her to rest and take the new tablets the GP had prescribed for her. She nodded to her son and left the room...

Callum was still gurgling away, as if he knew he was about to embark on a new journey down to the beach, Sandhaven Beach, it always looks magnificent whatever the season. Frankie would wrap him up well.

He placed him in the Silver Cross Pram, it was Emily's favourite, she picked it out. A stunning Navy Blue with Silver edgings....

He shouted back at his mam and dad,

'We are off now, for a wee stroll, won't be long'

His parents watched him through the living room window, and his dad made the comment,

'He is a natural, I cannot believe such a transformation since his visit to Church, I don't believe in his therapy with some counsellor to be honest pet', as he turned to his wife.

Agnes agreed and smiled back at him. Gerald got her comfortable and did the usual foot exercises with her, he was such a comfort to Agnes, always seeing to her needs. She felt so blessed and hoped these new tablets would help with her mobility. Ibuprofen she was told would certainly get her moving as it was a great painkiller...

The sun came out, and Frankie sang to his son as he strolled to the beach, they lived ten minutes away from the beach.

He would stroll along the promenade and Callum lay so comfortably, eyes wide open. 'Oh, was that a smile my son, it looked like a wee smile there', as he talked to his son...

Just as he approached the Promenade, Jason and Jacqueline were out for a morning stroll… Jacqueline immediately made her way to them as Jason followed her on…

'Oh, what a lovely surprise, Oh, my look at my wee Grandson, looking as handsome as ever'. Callum seem to smile at her…

Frankie conveyed his thoughts to her and began telling her how he had begun to settle a bit, cries a little, but I am right there when he cries. I talk to him a lot about Emily…

Jacqueline was a little taken back, she wasn't expecting him to talk of Emily, but she was happy that he did. She wanted to know more as they all sat down on the Promenade seat with shelter… it was getting a little breezy now…

Jason commented on how well he looked, and Frankie replied by saying,

'To be honest it was all Father Donnelly's doing, he brought me out of myself and got me to think of others and not dwell on things too deeply'.

Jacqueline commended Frankie for his efforts, and she knew that Father Donnelly would work wonders with him.

It was time they left as Frankie didn't want his son catching cold… As they said goodbye, Jacqueline looked on and relayed her thoughts to Jason.

'I think he has turned a corner, a good corner, I am so pleased for them. I just wish my Emily was here', as she got a little weepy.

Jason held onto her and changed the subject to relieve her of her sufferings for now. 'Right, young lady we are off to the farmhouse to see how our renovations are taking shape'.

Ronnie the Foreman had assembled his gang of men to formulate the alterations as per the specification from Jason himself. He wanted everything perfect for Jacqueline; he just didn't want anything to go wrong at this stage…

As they arrived at the farmhouse, Jason could see the house itself was taking shape and the annexed barn was looking fabulous for their wedding venue.

Roy informed him that it would take a further ten days to complete the work and it would be all theirs to move back into.

Jason was staying at Jacqueline's full time now, as the little annex attached to the farmhouse was a little cramped and Jacqueline suggested he move in with her… It just made perfect sense…

As they strolled around the house, Jason suggested they go and look for brand new furniture of her choice.

Jacqueline gazed around the rooms and began thinking of that chesterfield settee with its accompanied chesterfield armchair, and the large pouffe… The deep rustic brown would be ideal in the living room….

Jason could see Jacqueline's mind was working overtime as he looked at her and spoke,

'What have you been thinking of my love, I can see in her eyes' She smirked back at him and answered,

'You know that lovely Chesterfield we saw seems a long time back, but I think that would be ideal in this room. The set would be perfect because the armchair would sit nicely by the log fire… You chair maybe…'

Jason gave her a wry smile back and squeezed her waist before saying,

'You certainly know me, don't you, I can see the old armchair can go to the housekeeper as a going away present'

They made their way to Mason's in the Town Centre to the big furniture shop and browsed at the beautiful lamps and lampstands. The mahogany dining table and chairs caught Jacqueline's eye, because it had a hidden extension and you could extend it to fit ten people around the table...

Her thoughts drifted into a cosy family dinner with everyone, as she smiled down at it and touched the surface of the table...

Jason knew at that moment it was going to be an expensive afternoon, but he didn't care. He hadn't spent any monies on his home for years, and it was about time he did....

Jacqueline felt a sense of completeness as she sat on the chesterfield... It was beginning to feel like a new beginning.

Jason joined her on the settee and spoke

'This is the one, and the dining table and chairs. Oh, what about those lamps and lamps stands. Are we having the lot, I think we must, don't you'

She bent over and kissed him passionately; she didn't care at that moment that there were other people in the shop. Jason was stunned for moment but didn't mind it in the least. A man and woman walked by and the man, turned and winked at Jason... He laughed and looked towards Jacqueline... as she smiled back at the woman... who looked a little uncomfortable...

Jason moved towards the counter to pay his large bill and was told the delivery would be in ten days.... He was so happy with that...

They both decided to go for a celebratory drink in town, at the Majestic, it seemed fitting to do so on such an eventful day...

Jacqueline asked Jason if he didn't mind that she take a stroll to the cemetery later, alone. She wanted to talk to her Declan and tell him all her news and ask for his blessing, it was something she wanted to do for some time.

Jason told Jacqueline that she should go and have some quiet time, he didn't mind that at all. He admired Declan when he was alive, and felt he was honoured to take his place.

They arrived home and Jacqueline sauntered slowly to the cemetery it was a good stretch of walking, she needed that long walk to savour on her own, with her own thoughts.

She began thinking of the time they first arrived at the Cottage in South Shields back in 1943, as they had lived in a pit house along Hadrian Road before that. Her memories came flooding back to the time the children were born. It was Emily who was fragile one, and she spent more time with her than the others when they were little, but Emily grew to accept her asthma, she was feisty one at the age of five years...

The road seemed to be shorter than she had envisaged as she had reached her destination and was outside the cemetery gates...

The curve in the pathway took her to Declan's grave side... She stooped down with a bouquet of carnations, he loved them.

Her speech began...

'Hello, my love, I am here! with news! You already know about our dear Emily as she is with you, I know she is. I want to talk to you about Jason, you know him, he looked after you. Well, my love, he is so good and kind, and so generous. He loves me so dearest, and I do love him. It is not like us, but it's another kind of love that makes me so happy. I want your blessing my love, I need your blessing... you will give it... I know... because you are that kind of a man... Wish me luck my dearest. Bye for now'

She kissed the stone, and wept a little, tears of pain, and tears of joy.

The Woven Bliss, that loving kiss, it's sauntered memories flicker in the early mist....

Chapter 27

There was a kind of buzz surrounding the haberdashery shop on this brisk morning in Autumn. Belinda was overwhelmed with the response to a well-written advertisement in the local newspaper. It was Aileen who had placed it, and she too was pleased with the outcome.

They had interviewed over fifty applicants, and it was now time to call the applicants who were now shortlisted, seven of them in total.

Belinda was taken with Michelle's enthusiasm and her knowledge of book-keeping, knitting and patterns. She thought that Michelle could supervise the wool shop annexed to the haberdashery. It would give Belinda more time to manage the haberdashery section as it was growing in strength.

Aileen was concentrating on the handyman, and her thoughts were that Josh who had an outgoing personality with strong shoulders; he was her favourite.

They both put their heads together and came up with some questions they would like to ask each candidate, and they would then make their final decision.

The main question was,

'What would you do if you had an awkward encounter with a customer, how would you react'

They wanted a well-coordinated person who could work under pressure but remain calm in any altercation that may arise.

The interviews took place the next day, and Josh came out on top. Michelle also was well presented, organised and equipped to supervise the Wool Shop.

Charlotte, Serena's mam entered the shop, and Aileen was so happy see her. The conversation was enlightening to say the least, as Aileen became animated because Charlotte had come into the shop to enquire about the vacancy in the Art Shop, as she would dearly like to be considered. It did say part time and Charlotte was eager to engage in such a venture. After all she was a good painter and did have a diploma in Art.

Aileen hired her on the spot, and said,

'I knew you would answer the advert. I had tried telephoning you without success, and here you are. I am so pleased you walked through the door.

You were always going to be my first choice. Welcome abroad Charlotte. Let's have a cup of tea to celebrate, or perhaps a stronger drink if you prefer'

It was settled they would go to the bistro three doors down and have a liquid lunch to celebrate. Aileen would only have a small one, as she was driving. Charlotte agreed with that. She talked a lot about her art experience it was her favourite subject. She had some great ideas for the Art Shop. Aileen had no idea she was so creative.

Alistair, Charlotte's husband, was opposed to his wife working in a shop. He would keep that quiet at his law firm. He still had that snobbery instinct embodied in him.

She thought when Serena had married Dylan, he had gotten rid of such ideals, but the heated conversation they had the night before didn't seem so.

Charlotte was her own woman, and she would not back down, and Alistair always knew that. He admired her for it, but he wouldn't let her know that.

Serena, however, was elated for her mother and was a little envious as she had become so creative herself since having the twins, and she loved her life as it is for now...

The time will come to embark on the same journey as her mam, not while the children are growing. She couldn't bear to leave her babies.

The thought of returning to her father's law firm wasn't at all appealing to her at all….. Her whole life had completely changed since she had given birth to her children.

After their hearty lunch at the bistro, Aileen was so elevated that she made her way to Jacqueline's to give her the good news about the shops.

She felt it would be a good idea to keep this jovial atmosphere going by introducing an idea about the provincial hen party. It was not yet confirmed about the hen party as Jacqueline didn't feel it was appropriate at her age, she was so conventional, and old-fashioned. She felt hen parties were for the young.

Aileen, however, had other ideas. She had been to the Seahouses in the Community Hall a few months ago and saw lots of conventions and exhibitions… which were of the literary sense. It would make for a good outing as Jacqueline loved her literature…

She put it to Jacqueline, and she was not opposed to such an idea, she was quite impressed with her sister on this question.

It was settled; they would book an overnight stay at the Seahouses at their local Inn. It was reasonable. Jacqueline became excited about such a prospect, she felt quite young at girlish for a change… as she laughed with her sister.

Sara, her youngest sister, was on board for such a hen party. Bernadette too, she loved anything artistic.

Jacqueline wondered what Jason would do, but he had pointed out to her recently he wasn't that keen on a stag night. He didn't really have any close friends, just acquaintances as his whole life was his work at the hospital, and that seemed to fill a void. Jasper his dog became his comfort at home.

He was surprised at Jacqueline; she was so giddy with excitement as she talked to him that night about her hen night. It was as if he had forgotten about how good it was to feel young again, he was only forty-six. He was becoming stuck in his ways, and that night he had been awakened by Jacqueline, and it was doing him good as he became engrossed in the ideas from his future wife.

He spoke out later that night,

'Well, I suppose I could round up a few close colleagues and we could go off for a weekend of Golf to celebrate my up-and-coming nuptials'

Jacqueline gave him a wry smile, and answered 'You look younger by the minute by love'

He didn't know what to say to that but squeeze her tightly towards him.

It was time to talk about getting the pre wedding plans together. Jillian, her dearest friend from college was a great cake maker. She would approach her the next day. It would only be something simple with icing on, as she didn't want anything too fancy.

Jillian was so excited about such a request, but she wouldn't be doing anything plain for a dear friend. It would be a three-tier cake with her buttermilk filling, a sort of white velvet cake. It was one of her specialities…

Jason was great at organising the catering as he did so last Christmas. He felt that he would use the same people as they were excellent.

He would take care of the cars, and the flowers would be in the hands of Jacqueline.

Simon his old colleague was his best man, and Jacqueline would be given away by her dear son Colm, and Niamh would be her matron of honour.

The biggest headache for Jacqueline was that she hadn't decided on what to wear, would it be a beige suit, or pastel coloured suit, or should she go for an elegant dress with an attached jacket to it… She liked pillar box hats, and was thinking of a lace net over the hat would suffice…

She now that it was time to get the clothes sorted that very weekend as Jason had his suit fittings that Saturday….

It was time to visit Siobhan at 'Cazalet Elegant Wedding dresses', she had done such a great job for Emily and Frankie, and her outfits were exceptional...

Niamh was looking forward to the visit, she loved this quaint elegant shop, and you get a glass of champagne on arrival.

Siobhan greeted them with a warm smile, and her assistant gave them a glass of champagne. They sat together on the elegant French style settee and talked of design and their perfect idea of a suitable outfit.

As the dresses came forward to view, Siobhan was of the view that Jacqueline would suit a long dress, beige breaded with an attached jacket which looked rather elegant on the assistant wearing it...

Niamh pointed out that it would look gorgeous on her mam, and there was a lighter beige dress with a flowered petal design attached to the material which would be ideal for Niamh.

It was time for them to try on the dresses, as they both came out of their cubicles, Niamh was so impressed with her dress.

Jacqueline stood in her cubicle and was amazed at such a transformation she was exported to surreal moment of delight. Siobhan was so right, she had such great taste.

There were leaf-effect head pieces that had been handmade which complimented each dress.

They were all sold on the idea. Jacqueline hugged her daughter as they made their way to the full- blown mirrors that could visually see every side of you...

Jacqueline almost didn't want to take the dress she was looking at someone completely different in the mirror, and she liked that person she had become...

Shoes, ooh shoes I would just like a small thin heel, sling back for me.

Niamh liked her stilettoes ...

They sat and drank their champagne and Jacqueline invited Siobhan and her husband to the wedding. She was delighted to accept.

Jason and Simon were both wearing navy blue morning suits, they were tailored made. Simon made a gesture,

'I haven't worn a morning suit in my life, it feels quite unreal, but comfortable and I must admit I do look rather dapper'

Colm was in the background as he too was having the same attire, he loved his morning suit, and made a remark to Simon

'I too was like you Simon, this is my second time in a morning suit, and it's one of those moments when you think, yes, definitely be wearing one of these again.'

Jason asked Colm if he had ever played golf, Colm hadn't, but he did reply by saying, 'Hey, I can be your caddy man, I don't want to miss your stag night'

Jason hadn't thought of that, yes, great idea, they had a pre celebratory drink down the pub and Simon suggested that we could do with a few more on the stag night. Colm was only too happy to oblige and said that his Uncle Dylan would love a stag night and he would try and get Frankie to come along, but that might prove to be difficult because he has his hands full with little Callum. He could rustle a few of his mates if they were short in numbers.

Jason had a few colleagues from the hospital who were only too willing to participate, all in all, they are six.

The night was set for Friday night a week before the wedding… It wasn't going to be a boozy night, but you never know…

Jacqueline was still buzzing about her beautiful dress, it wasn't as beautiful as the white dress she wore for Declan, but this was special, and she knew it. It pleased her to think that way.

As she slipped into bed that night, she dreamt of Declan, but in a different way, they were talking about her future, and it soothed her to sleep feeling that warm contented feeling of fulfilment.

Chapter 28

As Autumn leaves lay, scattered along the crevices outside Frankie's house. He couldn't help but think of Emily on this cold windy day. It was Halloween coming up, and he remembered how Emily would decorate the place with lanterns and pumpkin ornaments. It was a test of their love that she tried new things out at home to get the right fit for the shop displays.

Her creative aspirations continued right up until Christmas... Frankie held Callum in his arms and told him of this narrative, and went on further to say,

'Now my wee lad, we will try making a pumpkin, just for you. All I need is a turnip, peel the inside and put a little candle there. I think I can manage that'. We will decorate the house with some lanterns. I know where they will be in the loft in Emily's special wooden chest'...

As they ventured to the local shop to buy some turnips, Frankie thought it best to buy at least three or four just make sure it got one right...

It felt strange to him getting back to his own home, but he wanted to get Callum settled before he went back to work... He would make this week special with a Halloween theme to light up the house.

Gerald and Agnes were so relieved that their son was finally finding his feet. Agnes thought it would be a good idea just to visit later that day just to make sure he was doing alright as mother's do. Gerald was of the view that he would be fine, but he gave in at the end, and they both decided to visit after tea.

In the meantime, Frankie had decided to go all out and get some lights to decorate the windows and mantlepiece. The six turnips he eventually bought turned out well.

The whole living room was alit with some of Emily's ornaments of autumn with various baubles made from pumpkins and a pumpkins house she designed herself...

As he stood back with Callum and looked on... Callum was looking all round at the lights and the little house seem to catch his eye, as Frankie told him of this story...

'Your beautiful mam sat me down and told me that she had designed this pumpkin house and the only thing missing was the lights. That was my job to fix, as I was good at that.... This little pumpkin house is now yours now my wee lad ...'

Colm and Bernadette pulled up outside his house and wondered what was going on, had they missed a party?

Frankie opened the door to him and took him inside. Colm and Bernadette were amazed at what they saw and asked Frankie what it was an aide of? And was he having a Halloween party. As they both looked at one another Frankie spoke,

'I saw the autumn leaves lay bare this morning outside and I thought of Emily and how she loved this season and how we use to decorate the house. I wanted to bring that back into the house for Callum to see'

Colm put his arm on Frankie's shoulder and answered,

'That is a wonderful thing you have achieved here today pal, our Emily is looking down on this and thinking my Frankie has done good'

They sat admiring the room for a moment and Colm had forgotten why he had called... It was Frankie who prompted him as he asked why the visit, checking up on me as he winked at Colm.

'I have come to ask if you wanted to come to Jason's stag weekend of golfing...

Frankie said he would love to, but he wanted time with Callum as he was going back to work the following Monday. He thanked him for the invite and would call

Jason to give him his best wishes, and he would have a drink with him at the wedding…

Agnes and Gerald arrived and were dumbfounded to see what a great effort their son had made. They were so proud of him and knew at the time he would be alright on his own.

Colm suggested that they call everyone and have that Halloween party and pre-drinks before the stag night, which was in a few days…

Emergency chairs were brought back from Gerald and Agnes's home to accommodate all the families…

Jason and Jacqueline arrived first, followed by Niamh and Jack and then Serena and Dylan with the twins… They had brought a whole car of accessories with them…

Jacqueline didn't come empty-handed as she had brought a selection of sandwiches and cakes and biscuits and brought sausages and burgers to cook.

 Frankie was ready for this family get-together it was just what the house needed. It was filled with joy and the remembrance of Emily who wouldn't have wanted it any other way…

The twins were put into the play pen and Callum watched on in his cradle, he was fascinated by their movements and gurgles, and he too would make his own gurgling sounds back to them…

As the food got underway, the smell in the kitchen was making Niamh a little queasy? She didn't want to have any attention paid upon her, so she made her way to the toilet... She was glad she wasn't physically sick, but the nausea seemed to have been with her for the past few days… and she noted her period was late by a week... but this had happened to her before, and she wasn't going to make a fuss. She washed her face and hands and patted herself on the thigh and smiled as she went back into the living room…

The food was served, and she stuck with the sandwiches... the men tucked into the burgers and sausages...

Jason had brought enough supplies of beer and wine... Agnes and Gerald stayed for a while, but it was passed their bedtime... at 9.30pm...

Jacqueline commented on her daughter's features as she turned to Niamh to say, 'You are looking a little peaky my pet, you need to get some vitamins in you, you work too hard at that school'. Jack looked at his wife and said,

'Yes, my love, you do look a little peaky'

Niamh got up to pour herself a drink and sharply answered her husband,

'Enough of that, I do have a pale complexion and yes, and sometimes I look a little pale. I will take my vitamins, don't worry'

Serena was the first to approach Niamh in the kitchen and she took her to one side and began telling her about how she felt before she found out she was pregnant.

Niamh could talk to Serena, and they both made their way to the patio outside. Serena spoke first,

'I know what you are thinking, and if I were you, I would go and see the doctor next week just to see what he has to say. I won't say a thing to anyone, not even Dylan until you say so....'

Niamh squeezed Serena's hand, and answered,

'Oh, thank you Serena, I have been feeling like this for a few days. I even felt faint yesterday and wondered if I was pregnant. You see, Jack and I, didn't take precautions when we were at the Lake District, so I might be'...

Serena asked if she would be happy if she was?? Niamh said she was scared at the prospect because she didn't feel she would be that good at it. As Serena turned Niamh to her, she spoke out ...

'You, my dear, will be a great mother, trust me, I am a Solicitor, I know these things...'

Niamh answered in a pleading manner,

'Oh Serena, would you help me! If I am! I am going to need all the help I can get!'

Serena laughed out loud,

'You will be absolutely fine'

The back door opened, and Dylan popped his head out and spoke,

'What is going on here then, such secrets?'

As he winked back at his wife.

Serena smiled at her husband and said,

'No secret, just us girls catching up, it's been an age since I last saw Niamh'

That statement seemed to deter any suspicions on their count. Niamh was relieved by the outcome. She bounced back to say,

'I have missed Serena and her wicked sense of humour; she always makes me laugh'

Dylan agreed and said his wife was full of wickedness when she wanted to be… They all joined the party and the conversation changed to the Stag night and Hen Party. Niamh was glad of such a diversion…

Jason was elevated about his Stag weekend, and Jacqueline was now becoming a little jealous of his jovial outbursts. She began saying...

'Our weekend at the Seahouses will be spectacular, for we have several projects on the go to keep us in the mood… and of course there is the banquet in the evening….'

Jason eyes rolled as he asked the question,

'What banquet, you never told me of a banquet'

Jacqueline smirked at her fiancé …

'Didn't I, oh, it must have slipped my mind' Dylan spoke,

'Do I detect a little rivalry of who is going to have the best night… I didn't realise that you two were so feisty'

Jason laughed and answered Dylan, 'You Ain't Seen Nothing Yet!'

Everyone in the room looked on and raised their eyebrows in a good way. They loved the way how Jason and Jacqueline had evolved and how they were so well suited to one another…

Colm and Bernadette sat back relishing their hopes of starting a family as they both played with the twins and watched Callum who was fast asleep at this point… They had been trying for a baby but no success yet… it was early days, Colm kept thinking to himself…

He was feeling a little worried that they hadn't conceived and wondered if there was anything wrong…. His thoughts were that he should go to the Doctors and ask the question, but he had been too scared to approach Bernadette with his fears. Instead, he wanted them to just keep on trying for now…. No need to panic at this stage he felt….

Chapter 29

What a morning of disarray, as they all prepared for their weekend of partying.... Niamh was in the bathroom, being sick and Jack was busy sorting his golf clubs, they belonged to his dad, he was happy to take them... He had played golf with his father on occasion but hadn't played in the last year. He was whistling away in the shed outside and didn't notice Niamh's predicament in the bathroom.

She was determined to get herself together as she was looking forward to her weekend at the sea houses. As she washed her face and got her assembled to look as though nothing had occurred.

'This is not going to affect me, not now', as she whispered to herself in the mirror...

Jacqueline was all of dither and couldn't get herself assembled at all; she couldn't make her mind up what to put in her small suitcase.

Her sisters arrived, Aileen and Sara, they looked on at Jacqueline and couldn't help but laugh out loud as they both spoke together...

'Look at you our Jacques, you a like a nervous teenager, goodness knows how you are going to be on the wedding day. We will have to steer you in the right direction'

Jacqueline huffed and puffed and answered back,

'Really, you two, I don't, think so, I can manage... I just need to get myself better organised that's all'

Her sister's raised their eyebrows and smirked at one another before getting a little celebration on the go before they were off on their journey.... Drinks were ready to be poured, and Serena had arrived just in time... She had dropped the twins off at her mums.

The minibus would arrive in twenty minutes, so they all had time to have that drink of champagne Aileen had brought along with her.

Jacqueline informed the driver that there were two more passengers to pick up on the way, Niamh and Bernadette.

Jason had organised his minibus, as he had packed up his belongings, which included lots of golf clubs and golf balls, enough for everyone....

All the boys had arrived at Jason's, and they were all excited to get off to Golf Course. They would stay at the Sunshine Inn near Whitburn.

The weekend got off to a great start, and the boys got themselves settled at the Inn. Jason informed everyone that a good round of golf is the best medicine and then we can have a liquid lunch to celebrate after...

Dylan and Colm thought it was a little conservative and were planning to make this a proper stag night... Jack too was in on this conversation....

Jason's colleagues, had opted for the suitable liquid lunch afterwards... It looked like it was going to be a divided stag party...

Dylan nodded to Jack and Colm and spoke,

'Early days, lads, early days... let's just go with the flow for now'

Whilst the girls, were having a ball at the sea houses, there were so many exhibitions in the Community Hall, Painting, making paper figurines, and there was cross stitching... an assortment of knitted toys and accessories... Serena was in her element in that corner...

Jacqueline opted for the poetry corner as she sat with a group who were writing their own poem and then after everyone had written theirs. The group would debate each poem on merit and content... She was transfixed in that corner...

Sara and Aileen were happy in the arts and crafts section as browsed around and took a drink in the bar annexed to the hall... That was their way of thinking today... They would grab Jacqueline in a few hours to join them...

Niamh and Bernadette were happy with all the paintings as they studied the selection. It was Niamh who spoke first, enquiring about how Bernadette was, and she was still enjoying the wedding bliss. She asked the question about having a family.

Bernadette sat down on the stool next to her and beckoned Niamh to sit on the stool next to her as she began her tale of worries.

'We have been trying for a baby for ages, but nothing has happened. Do you think we should go to the GP and ask if there is anything they can recommend?

Niamh startled by it all, began answering...

'Well, I don't think it will do any harm, it may put your mind at rest. Best if you both go together'

Bernadette asked the same question to Niamh and her reply took Bernadette by complete surprise!

'To be honest Bernadette, I think I am pregnant, I am late, and I have been suffering with nausea for the past week. I have an appointment at the Doctors on Monday. Please don't say anything; there is only Serena that suspects... I can't believe I have told you, I haven't even told Jack yet. I am waiting to see what the Doctor says first before I tell him'

Bernadette assured Niamh she would not tell anyone about this conversation; she couldn't help but feel a little envious... Hoping one day that will be her....

The morning of activities had gone well. Aileen and Sara got everyone together in the bar and they all had drinks. Niamh stuck to sparkling water, and her mam couldn't help but notice...

Before she could question her daughter about it, Sara diverted her to accept a cocktail to her liking... She wanted one with lots of fruit, but not so much alcohol.... She made sure she got what she wanted she gave firm instructions to the barman.

The evening Banquet in the Hall was a success, such a large selection of foods to sample. Jacqueline was so surprised at how many selections there were. There were cheeses she hadn't even heard of but tried them anyway...

The boys golfing was coming to an end, and they all made their way to the Inn. Dylan and Jack were happy about that, so was Colm. He felt caddying was a heavy job, but he felt fitter for the exercise, energised even. He was ready for his liquid lunch.

There was a band on that night, so it looked like they could have a proper stag night... A rock and roll band that brought the house down.

It turned out that Jason's colleagues were not as reserved as they thought, they became rather rowdy and drank quite a lot... Jason too had let his guard down and it was a night to remember.... It may not be the next morning for some...

The girl's night was full of laughter and memories, and Jacqueline couldn't have wished for a better time... They would go out on Sunday to take in the views. Jacqueline would visit church first thing, before embarking on their home return...

Sunday had arrived and the hangovers for the men were prominent in everyone's room... As Jason awoke, he was suffering with an awful feeling of nausea and sprang to the bathroom. He had never drunk that much in his life; his colleagues however had drunk the bar dry...

Their day of another round of golf was never happening... They had all day to recuperate until the minibus arrived at 6pm....

Dylan and Jack looked across at Jason as they mounted the minibus... to say 'You did have a great time, Jason; you were up dancing and singing'...

Jason had recalled dancing, but couldn't remember the singing part of it... He smiled at the lads and said,

'It's a first, and it's my last'...

They all seemed to sleep their way home....

The girls however, they were jolly, and full of conversation on their way home and Jacqueline went towards her Niamh... she wanted to ask the question...

'Hey pet, did you have good time, are you alright, you didn't drink an ounce of alcohol... Is this what I think it is?'

Niamh looked at her mam,

'I see the GP in the morning mam, please don't say anything. I am telling Jack after I have been to see the GP.'

Jacqueline hugged her daughter and whispered.

'I wouldn't do that pet; do you want me to come with you,' Niamh smiled with a relieved expression on her face as she answered,

'Oh, yes, please mam, it is at 10.15am. Pick you up at 10'

Her mam told her that when she goes to the toilet first thing, take a little bottle with you and fill it. The GP will then send it off to the hospital for a positive test, or a negative test. As she turned to her daughter with a caring look on her face

'In your case, my pet, I think it will be positive,'

Monday morning came so quickly, and Niamh was up at 6am... Jack was so surprised to see her up so soon... She made the excuse that she had lots to organise at the school before end of term... He accepted that and kissed her on the mouth and left for work.

She sauntered around... the classroom and got another teacher to cover for her. The drive to the GP's was quicker than she thought, as she pulled up in the carpark Jacqueline told her not to be too nervous...

They sat for five minutes, and then Niamh's name was called to see Dr Castle. He examined Niamh and asked the usual questions... He took the sample from her and began saying...

'I would say you are about eight weeks pregnant; I am sure the sample will come back as positive, which I should have in a possession within forty-eight hours... Any questions?'

Niamh sat motionless... at first and answered back,

'Thank you, Doctor, do I just telephone for the results, or do you telephone me?'

Dr Castle informed Niamh that he would telephone her on Wednesday at 9am. She would make a point of going to work later that morning... It was Wednesday and she had free period as no lessons for two hours, just planning to take care. She would do that the night before...

As they got into the car Jacqueline told her daughter to talk to Jack tonight,

'You must pet. Niamh nodded to her mam...

Jacqueline was wondering if this was good news... or not... Niamh said that she hadn't really planned it, but she was a little excited... just scared a little too... as she spoke to her mam.

Her mam told her to stop the car, and she pulled in.

'Now pet, you will make a fabulous mam, you will, I know you will, don't worry, you have your family to help you through the scary parts'

It was time to tell Jack... She set the table with candles and made a special steak dinner in the hope that the news would excite him too

As he walked through the door, he looked at the table and glanced towards the table, and looked at Niamh with a bemused look on his face, he was thinking he had missed an important date? He couldn't think of a thing, as he scratched his head and spoke first,

'What is this my pet, are we celebrating something?'

Niamh guided him to his chair and gave him a beer and spoke calmly,

'Yes, my love; you know our nights of passion at the Lake District... it turned out to be more memorable than we had thought... We are pregnant, I think. Doc says so, but my urine test won't be back until Wednesday to confirm.'

Jack startled by this amazing statement as he put his bottle of beer down, he picked up his wife and spun her around and shouted out loud,

'We are pregnant, I am one happy man'

The news on Wednesday confirmed the pregnancy and Niamh's life was to change once more....

A woven bliss that threads the new and a love is born so true....

Chapter 30

Jason and Jacqueline spent their last few hours together before the Wedding Day! It was fast approaching... and Jason looked down at his wife to be and kissed her gently before saying,

'Any regrets?'

Jacqueline responded with a warm embrace,

'The only regret is that I lead you a merry dance leaving you wandering if I would'

Jason held her in his arms and spoke softly,

'My love for you, it stood the test of time, I knew you just needed time'

They sat outside in the garden at Jacqueline's cottage and had their quiet moment before Jason had to set off to his home. He left Jacqueline in the garden as she reminisced about times gone by. As she smiled at herself, she had no regrets, just the sadness of those she had lost...

Her life was to change, and she was ready for that change, and embraced it with all her heart.

The doorbell rang, it was her sisters, followed by Niamh and Jack, Colm and Bernadette. Jacqueline was so surprised, she advised everyone that this is not party night, that's for tomorrow night...

Niamh and Jack stepped forward and announced that they were pregnant. Jacqueline hugged them both, followed by Aileen and Sara. Colm stood back stunned but went forward eventually to kiss his sister and wish her all the best.

Bernadette whispered in her ear,

'I knew you were, you will be a great mum'.

Colm and Bernadette left the house early... as Colm wanted to talk to Bernadette and tell her not to worry about conceiving. He told her that if they could not have a child of their own, they would adopt and that would be that...

Bernadette tearful at this point, squeezed his arm and then changed the subject to the wedding... They had to wrap up the wedding presents; it was a nestle of oak tables that Colm knew his mam would love. He thought they would go lovely with the oak furniture Jason had in the adjoining sitting room next to his living room.

The morning of wedding was rather chaotic in everyone's household... Niamh had slept in a little and Aileen and Sara were stuck in traffic...

Jacqueline sighed a little and muttered to herself,

'It's just as well, the wedding doesn't start until 3pm, thank goodness for that... As she sat alone in her living room with a cup of tea... She had plenty of time to get to the hairdressers, as it was just down the road...

As she ventured out, she caught sight of her sisters and gave out a relieved shout out...

'Aww you got here then'

Niamh arrived at the hairdressers half an hour after everyone... As they all got themselves organised to go back to Jacqueline's... Niamh had forgotten to put her shoes in the car.... Aileen told her to 'sit tight, don't want you to get nauseated.... I will fetch them'

Jason and the boys, however, were so co-ordinated, they were ready hours before the service....

Dylan suggested a game of poker, to pass the time away... as they sat in the back of church... It was Jason who decided to set off early.... He wasn't taking any chances on the traffic...

Aileen and Sara helped Jacqueline into her dress and stood back with admiration for their oldest sister.... Sara spoke,

'You look a picture our Jacques'

Jacqueline wanted to be alone for five minutes, as she got out Declan's picture, she sat talking to him... She even imagined he was smiling down at her, which soothed her so....

They were already to go, and wedding cars had arrived... Colm escorted his mam in the bridal car with pride in his eyes, and the girls followed on....

Father Donnelly interrupted the boys in the back as he opened the door, his eyebrows raised with a smirk on face...

'Now then, it's time to take your place in the front of the Altar, everyone is arriving...'

Jason looked a little embarrassed as he put his cards down and nodded to Father Donnelly. He just winked back at him....

Clarice the soprano was to sing Ave Maria and Fred was on the organ playing as Jacqueline came down the Aisle, she loved that hymn... It was her preference when entering the church...

The service was lengthy, Jason didn't realise you would have to kneel so much... but he didn't mind, he had the love of his life next to him, and he would kneel all day if he had to.

The photographers were ready and there was a big crowd outside as Jacqueline was well known at St Bernadettes, they had come along to wish her well and throw their confetti... There was a lot of confetti thrown!! As they darted in and out to the bridal car....

Jason smoothed over Jacqueline face as it was covered... with white and pink confetti.... The wedding party were on their way to Jason's Barn where the venue was all set up...

The renovations and décor were to Jason's liking, and the catering did not disappoint... There was to be trio' The Magpies' who played classical music as well as pop...

Father Donnelly stepped out of his comfort zone and attended the meal... He wanted to raise a glass to

Jacqueline and Jason, as he had known her for such a long time and seen her go through so much. It was an honour to accept the invitation. Jacqueline was over the moon about his presence and let him know that...

Everyone enjoyed themselves, and little Callum was happy to stay awake watching all the activities and gurgling towards the twins next to him. They all seemed to love the music.

The wedding day couldn't go any better, and Jason and Jacqueline set off for their weekend Honeymoon in the Cotswolds... She always wanted to go to visit the Cathedral there. Also, the arts and crafts they were famous for... They would stay in a quaint Inn near the Cathedral....

Jason had organised it all and made sure they had everything sent up to their rooms, Champagne, truffles, and a bouquet of Mixed Roses.... He wanted everything just right for Jacqueline...

They would wander the Cotswolds, taking in the idyllic views of the rolling hills, which were so romantic.

They had the most blissful time in the Cotswolds, and Jacqueline turned to her husband as they were about to set off home and began her little speech,

'I never thought I would ever be as happy again, but you have made me realise that there is a second chance and it is as good as the first, I love you so much'

Jason looked at his wife with tears in his eyes and spoke out...

'You are so beautiful, and I think that I will never forget those words as long as I live'

She lay her head on his shoulder as he drove them home...

Back home, Colm and Bernadette plucked up the courage to visit the GP's, and they had the tests scheduled for the next day.

It turned out that the GP was right there was nothing wrong they were just trying too hard, they needed to step back and let it happen naturally....

Niamh was having a time of it with nausea, and she was given some sickness tablets which seem to ease it a little... She was so happy, it did not annoy her too much, as she was now embracing the idea of motherhood...

Jack couldn't wait for the day... ... The lads down the pit couldn't get him to stop smiling... They reminded him, the smile would disappear when he was to experience those sleepless nights. He just laughed at them all...

As the months went by, Niamh became bigger, and her mam pointed out that she was probably having a boy she thought.... ....

On the night of the birth, Niamh had become so cramped all day, but she hadn't realised she was having contractions...

Jack was well organised; he had the overnight bag all set to go.... and he had her in the car before she could blink... When they arrived at the hospital she was taken straight down to the delivery suite.

Mr Robson was surprised she hadn't come in earlier, but it look like Niamh was going to deliver quickly, she wasn't in labour long when she arrived...

Baby Sarah Louise was born, 8lbs 12 oz. She was a lovely bonny baby, crying her lungs out...

Jason and Jacqueline arrived... they couldn't believe it! How did this happen so quickly. Jack pointed out that she had cramped all day, and we didn't realise they were contractions…....

Jacqueline laughed and said,

'That's a good way to have an easy birth, proud of you my pet', as she kissed her daughter.

Colm and Bernadette arrived, and they too were so surprised. Colm commented on how big baby Sarah was...

Niamh laughed at her brother and answered... 'Tell me about it! bro, she was heavy going'....

They left Niamh to get some well-deserved rest, as the nurse took baby Sarah to the baby's room...

Colm suggested they went for drink to wet the baby's head so to speak.... They all decided to go ... and Colm called Dylan to come along too.

It was whilst they were in the pub, Jacqueline had a quiet word with her son to see how they were doing...

Colm said he was confident that it would be their turn before long.... And he was right...

Five months later, Bernadette became pregnant, and she delivered a baby boy, Daniel 7lb 4oz ...

Everyone was settling into their new way of life. Jason and Jacqueline had their routine down to a tee. Jason would sleep over at the hospital when on nights, to get a good sleep in between his call outs.... whilst Jacqueline looked after Callum in the daytime.

They were well organised, and Jason loved his evenings and weekends with his new bride...

Frankie too was happy to be back at the garage and looked forward to picking up his son Callum...

The pain they had all endured, had gone by like a misty spray over the sea, they all took comfort in their newfound lives....

The Woven Bliss its joy so sweet.... It's love so complete.......

www.ingramcontent.com/pod-product-compliance
Lightning Source LLC
Chambersburg PA
CBHW052027070526
44584CB00016B/1935

Echoes from the Higher Ground

Combining
The Mountain Still Speaks
Volume II: Still He Speaks -
The Narrow Way, the Secret
Life, and the Rock That Stands

DAMIANO B. CENTOLA

EXPLORA BOOKS
700 – 838 West Hastings St. Vancouver
BC V6C 0A6
www.explorabooks.com
Phone: (604) 330 6795

No part of this book may be reproduced, stored in a retrieval system, or transmitted by any means without the written permission of the author.

Because of the dynamic nature of the Internet, any web addresses or links contained in this book may have changed since publication and may no longer be valid. The views expressed in this work are solely those of the author and do not necessarily reflect the views of the publisher, and the publisher hereby disclaims any responsibility for them.

Bible verses are quoted from the King James Version (KJV), which is public domain, the English Standard Version (ESV), and the New King James Version (NKJV).

ISBN: 978-1-83430-038-*2 (Paperback)*
978-1-83430-039-9 *(Hardback)*
978-1-83430-040-5 *(eBook)*

© 2025 Damiano B. Centola. All rights reserved.